The Christian Life

The Christian Life

H. GUY MOORE

Convention Press

NASHVILLE   TENNESSEE

© 1961 • CONVENTION PRESS
Nashville, Tennessee

511–00103

Church Study Course
This book is 0103 in category 1, section for Adults and Young People

Library of Congress Catalog Card Number: 61–11985
Printed in the United States of America
15. AL 61 R.R.D.

About the Author

H. GUY MOORE was born at Du Quoin, Illinois, in 1909. He is a graduate of William Jewell College, Liberty, Missouri, having received the A.B. degree in 1931 and the D.D. degree in 1945. He is a graduate of Southern Baptist Theological Seminary, Louisville, Kentucky, having received the Th.M. degree in 1934.

In 1931 he was married to Miss Myron Catherine O'Dell of Excelsior Springs, Missouri. They have four children—David, Rodney, Nancy, and Robert.

Dr. Moore has served the following churches: Leeds Baptist Church, Kansas City, Missouri, 1934–36; Maplewood Baptist Church, St. Louis, Missouri, 1936–40; Wornal Road Baptist Church, Kansas City, Missouri, 1940–47. Since 1947 he has been pastor of the Broadway Baptist Church in Fort Worth, Texas.

He served as chairman of the committee on world evangelization of the Southern Baptist Convention, as a member of the Home Mission Board and the board of trustees of William Jewell College, Southwest Baptist College, and Mary Hardin-Baylor College, and is a member of the Christian Life Commission of Texas. He is presently a member of the Baptist Radio and Television Commission.

Dr. Moore is a frequent speaker at the Baptist assemblies at Ridgecrest and Glorieta and has contributed to two books, *Christian Faith in Action* and *Southern Baptist Preaching*, and also numerous publications of the Sunday School Board.

Dr. Moore has traveled extensively. He attended the Baptist World Alliance in Copenhagen, Denmark, 1947, and toured Europe. He accompanied Dr. Frank Means, of the Foreign Mission Board, in 1953, on a tour of Southern Baptist mission stations in Nigeria, Ghana, Southern Rhodesia, Lebanon, Syria, the Holy Land, and Europe. He addressed the Baptist World Alliance in London, England, in 1955. He attended the Baptist World Alliance in Rio de Janeiro, Brazil, in 1960, and toured several of the countries of South America.

Church Study Course

THE CHURCH STUDY COURSE began October 1, 1959. It is a merger of three courses previously promoted by the Sunday School Board —the Sunday School Training Course, the Graded Training Union Study Course, and the Church Music Training Course. On October 1, 1961, the Woman's Missionary Union principles and methods studies were added.

The course is fully graded. The system of awards provides a series of five diplomas of twenty books each for Adults or Young People, two diplomas of five books each for Intermediates, and two diplomas of five books each for Juniors. Book awards earned previously in the Sunday School Training Course, the Graded Training Union Study Course, and the Church Music Training Course may be transferred to the new course.

The course is comprehensive, with books grouped into twenty categories. The purpose of the course is to help Christians to grow in knowledge and conviction, to help them to grow toward maturity in Christian character and competence for service, to encourage them to participate worthily as workers in their churches, and to develop leaders for all phases of church life and work.

The Church Study Course is promoted by the Baptist Sunday School Board, 127 Ninth Avenue, North, Nashville, Tennessee, through its Sunday School, Training Union, Church Music, and Church Administration departments; and the Woman's Missionary Union, 600 North Twentieth Street, Birmingham, Alabama; and by the respective departments in the states affiliated with the Southern Baptist Convention. A complete description of the course and the system of awards may be found in the catalog, *Church Study Course,* which may be obtained without charge from any one of these departments.

A record of all awards earned should be maintained in each church. A person should be designated by the church to keep the files. Forms for such records may be ordered from any Baptist Book Store.

Requirements for Credit in Class
or Home Study

IF CREDIT IS DESIRED for the study of this book in a class or in home study the following requirements must be met:

I. IN CLASSWORK

1. The class must meet a minimum of seven and one-half clock hours. The required time does not include assembly periods. Ten class periods of forty-five minutes each are recommended. (If laboratory or clinical work is desired in specialized or technical courses, this requirement may be met by six clock hours of classwork and three clock hours of supervised laboratory or clinical work.)

2. A class member who attends all class sessions and completes the reading of the book within a week following the last class session will not be required to do any written work.

3. A class member who is absent from one or more sessions must answer the questions on all chapters he misses. In such a case, he must turn in his paper within a week, and he must certify that he has read the book.

4. The teacher should request an award for himself. A person who teaches a book in the section for Intermediates or Juniors of any category or conducts an approved unit of instruction for Nursery, Beginner, or Primary children will be granted an award in category 11, Special Studies, which will count as an elective on his own diploma. He should specify in his request the name of the book taught or the unit conducted for Nursery, Beginner, or Primary children.

5. The teacher should complete the "Request for Book Awards—Class Study" (Form 150) and forward it within two weeks after the completion of the class to the Church Study Course Awards Office, 127 Ninth Avenue, North, Nashville 3, Tennessee.

II. IN HOME STUDY

1. A person who does not attend any class session may receive credit by answering all questions for written work as indicated in the book. When a person turns in his paper on home study, he must certify that he has read the book.

2. Students may find profit in studying the text together, but individual papers are required. Carbon copies or duplicates in any form cannot be accepted.

3. Home study work papers may be graded by the pastor or a person designated by him, or they may be sent to the Church Study Course Awards office for grading. The form "Request for Book Awards—Home Study" (Form 151), must be used in requesting awards. It should be mailed to Church Study Course Awards Office, 127 Ninth Avenue, North, Nashville 3, Tennessee.

III. CREDIT FOR THIS BOOK

This book is No. 0103 in category 1, section for Adults and Young People.

Suggested Audio-Visual Aids
for Teaching This Book

SEVERAL SUGGESTIONS are given. The teacher is not expected to use all of them, but to choose the ones that are suitable. The teacher may want to add to, or change the suggestions.

A filmstrip, *The Christian Life* (26b) 52 frames, color, with two manuals, $5.00, has been prepared to be used as a teaching tool. The frame numbers will appear by each chapter number below.

CHAPTER 1 (frames 3-9)

HIDDEN CHALKBOARD: List the seven questions in third paragraph on a chalkboard. Cover each question with adding machine tape or dry-wall tape. Introduce the study of this book by exposing the questions one at a time.

CHALKBOARD: Write the following questions as they are discussed. I. What was God's purpose in creation? II. What kind of creature was he? III. Did man fulfil God's purpose in creation? and IV. Will God's plan be fulfilled?

FILMSTRIP: *God's Wonderful World*—(23c) 69 frames, color, with manual. $5.50

CHAPTER 2 (frames 10-14)

SLIDE: Obtain a slide or flat picture of Michelangelos' painting mentioned in part I of this chapter. The flat picture could be projected in an opaque projector.

FLIP CHART: Prepare a flip chart to be used several times throughout the book. If nothing else is available use the want ad section of a newspaper and liquid shoe polish to make the chart. On the first three sheets put the following wording: (1) What man must know—that Christian life cannot begin without a knowledge and en-counter with Jesus Christ; (2) What a man must do—repent; and (3) What a man must believe—that God is.

FILMSTRIPS: *What Baptists Believe About Salvation*—(26b) 50 frames, color, with two manuals, $5.50. Recording optional, $2.50

MOTION PICTURE: *Newness of Life*—14 minutes, rental $4.00

CHAPTER 3 (frames 15-18)

FILMSTRIP: *What Baptists Believe About Christian Growth and Service*—(26b) 50 frames, color, with two manuals, $5.00

FRIEZE: Make a picture map as described in Roman numeral II. Show the warfare of *The Christian Life*. Use some of Bunyans' "enemies" to make the map interesting.

MOTION PICTURE: *Unto A Full Grown Christian*—29 minutes, rental $9.00

CHAPTER 4 (frames 19-23)

FLIP CHART: On the fourth sheet of the flip chart draw a chart comparing the time and effort spent on the mental and physical development of our children as compared to the time spent on the spiritual development of our children.

POSTER: Take the wording under Roman numeral III, chapter 4 outline and make a poster from it.

MODEL: Obtain or make a model church.

FLIP CHART: On the next page of the flip chart put at the top, "What Can I Do." Then list below the following things: (1) Pray (2) Give (3) Serve (4) Influence

MOTION PICTURE: *My Church*—10 minutes, color, rental $5.00

FILMSTRIP: *What Baptists Believe About the Church*—(26b) 50 frames, color, with two manuals $5.50. Recording optional, $2.50

CHAPTER 6 (frames 28-38)

FLIP CHART: On another sheet put the following statement at the top: "The Meaning of God's Kingdom." Then list the following: (1) It is moral; (2) It is spiritual; and (3) It is actual.

On the next sheet put the seven Beatitudes as they are given in Roman numeral II. On still another sheet list the following: A Christian's conduct—(1) is characterized by righteousness, (2) must give attention to his motives, (3) must weigh the values of life, and (4) must be governed by moral discernment.

OBJECT: Add to the model church already on display a burning candle and a basket.

CHAPTER 7 (frames 39-46)

FILMSTRIPS: *Training Union and Stewardship* (26b) 39 frames, color, $5.00. *Wittness to the World* (26b) 46 frames, color, with manual $5.00. Recording available.

MOTION PICTURES: *Every Christian a Missionary*—14 minutes, rental $6.00, color $9.00. *My Job or A Calling*—28 minutes, rental $9.00

CHAPTER 8 (frames 47-52)

OBJECT: Add a cross to the objects and model already on display.

FILMSTRIP: *If God Be for Us*—(26b) 43 frames, color, $5.00. Recording available.

MOTION PICTURE: *Triumphant*—17 minutes, rental $6.00, color $9.00
The Way of Peace—18 minutes, rental, $6.50

Contents

The Christian Life

CHAPTER 1 OUTLINE

I. THIS CREATED WORLD

    1. The World of Nature

    2. The Crown of Creation

    3. Man in This Vast Universe

II. THE MAN GOD MADE

    1. God Made Man in His Image

    2. God Made Man Responsive

    3. God Made Man Responsible

    4. God Made Man Immortal

III. THE BROKEN IMAGE

    1. The Problem of Evil

    2. The Confidence of God

    3. The Riddle of the Universe

IV. THE UNFOLDING PURPOSE

    1. God's Purpose in Hebrew History

    2. God's Purpose in All History

    3. God's Purpose in Making Man

    4. God's Purpose Fulfilled in Christ

1

God's Eternal Purpose—
the New Creation

"In the beginning God . . ." (Gen. 1:1). With these majestic words our Bible begins. For here is the ultimate Reality— the source of all things. That marks for us the beginning of the cosmic order. It is the beginning of life. But we cannot stop there. The next word is not incidental—it is essential. It is essentially at one with all that goes before and all that is to follow. The word is *created*—"In the beginning God *created* . . ." Or it may read, "When God began to create . . ."

All that follows flows like a fountain of water from a mountain stream. Pouring from some higher source, it must flow. It is the nature of things as they are. God being who he is must create. Life cannot remain in the past tense. The God with whom we have to do has acted, he is acting, he will continue to act. Jesus said, "My Father has continued working until now, and I am working, too" (John 5:17, Montgomery). Creation is not a finished story. As there was the beginning in God, so there can and will be new beginnings. As life began with him, so new life can begin. His purpose for life is a continuing purpose.

What is that purpose for life—a life, yours and mine? Why did God make us? Why did he make us as he did? What did he have in mind for us? Is there a way we can know? Has any life ever achieved God's maximum purpose for it? How and where can we find fulfilment of God's purpose for us?

That shall be the concern of this book. By his grace we shall seek for the fulfilment of his purpose in the new creation—the new life in Christ.

3

I. This Created World

What was God's purpose in creation? To know the complete answer to that is too much to expect of finite minds. We know the beginnings. We see the unfolding process. We look toward the fulfilment. The beginning, the process, the fulfilment—each implies a purpose. If the understanding is ever given us to know, we must await the outcome, for it is the outcome that reveals the hidden purpose of the origin. Now, for a moment we look at the beginning.

1. *The World of Nature*

"In the beginning God created the heaven and the earth" (Gen. 1:1). So far as we are concerned you cannot improve upon that statement. With one majestic sentence the origin of this universe and all created things is defined.

Then they follow—sweeping, breath-taking descriptions of unequaled grandeur. God's creative acts tumble over one another, leaving us standing in awe. "The earth was without form, . . ." (Gen. 1:2). And then we go from chaos to order, from darkness to light, from lifelessness to living things. And again and again he surveys his work and says, "It is good!"

Can we doubt that? Wherever we look—from the farthest star to the tiniest flower, to the inner world of the atom—we find our finest mood in the spirit of praise. "The heavens declare the glory of God; and the firmament sheweth his handywork. Day unto day uttereth speech, and night unto night sheweth knowledge. There is no speech nor language, where their voice is not heard" (Psalm 19:1–3).

This is my Father's world, and to my list'ning ears,
All nature sings, and round me rings the music of the spheres,
This is my Father's world, I rest me in the thought
Of rocks and trees, of skies and seas His hand the wonders wrought.

2. *The Crown of Creation*

However good and beautiful the world of created things, it could not satisfy the creative urge of the God of life. There must be something yet greater. There must be life akin to his life. The God of life would make something *after his kind!* "And God said, Let us make man in our image, after our likeness: . . ." (Gen. 1:26). Creative life must create its kind. Creative love must create someone to be loved and to love in return. Neither God nor man can live by bread alone —nor for the glory of things. So man becomes both the crown and the goal of creation.

How beautifully does Mrs. Billy Graham put it in her Christmas story. "God loved the things he had made. But he had no children to share them with him. In all the earth, there was no one like himself, no one to say, 'How beautiful it is!' To have a companion on earth, God needed someone like himself. So he made our kind of creature and he made it in his own image . . . For God loved Adam and Eve so much that every evening at the close of the long, happy day, he came into the garden and talked with them. And then— new joy on earth!—the man and the woman answered him. It was the moment God had waited for since time began. 'At last,' he thought, 'I have my children.'" [1]

3. *Man in This Vast Universe*

There is a story of the student who took a photograph of a mountain pass in Switzerland. "When this was developed, there appeared in it, part of the way up the long, sinuous mountain trail, the solitary figure of a man, all but lost among the peaks. The photograph, which was to have shown the majesty of the mountains, became far more significant because of the man struggling up the slippery crag." [2]

---

[1] References listed on page 142.

That is the symbol of man in this expanding universe—lonely, afraid, struggling, but always climbing toward some distant goal. He is dwarfed by the vastness which surrounds him, and yet, the vastness has no significance without him. He is the point of reference in this universe. Man was not, therefore, an afterthought of God. He was in the plan. Indeed, he was at the very heart of the plan. In him creation attains a moral and a spiritual level. He is the connecting link between the material and the spiritual universe. All else must be interpreted in terms of man—under God. God's purpose will move forward with man in mind. "So God created man in his own image, in the image of God created he him; male and female created he them. And God blessed them, and God said unto them, Be fruitful, and multiply, and replenish the earth, and subdue it: and have dominion over the fish of the sea, and over the fowl of the air, and over every living thing that moveth upon the earth" (Gen. 1:27–28).

It was God who set man front and center on the stage of this vast universe.

II. THE MAN GOD MADE

Since man was to hold such a place of importance—second only to God in this world—what kind of a creature was he? The question of the psalmist becomes our question: "When I consider thy heavens, the work of thy fingers, the moon and the stars, which thou hast ordained; what is man, that thou art mindful of him? and the son of man, that thou visitest him? For thou hast made him a little lower than the angels, and hast crowned him with glory and honour. Thou madest him to have dominion over the works of thy hands; thou hast put all things under his feet" (Psalm 8:3–6).

1. God Made Man in His Image

This is the first descriptive word in the Bible concerning man—"Let us make man in our image, after our likeness"

(Gen. 1:26). Would that we could know all that that implies.

There are many conflicting views concerning man in our contemporary thought today. Our interest, however, is in the biblical, Christian point of view. That which distinguishes our Hebrew-Christian faith is that man is made in the image of God, not gods in the images of men. It is the movement of revelation—God to man, not man to God. This does not mean that we bear likeness to God in our physical bodies. Physically, we are in many respects like other animals. The thing that sets us apart from all others and makes us akin to God is our spiritual nature and quality. "And the Lord God formed man of the dust of the ground, and breathed into his nostrils the breath of life; and man became a living soul" (Gen. 2:7).

So man is both a body and a soul. In his physical nature he is akin to God's created, physical world. In his spiritual nature he bears the stamp of the very life of God who is spirit. In every human soul there is a God-shaped blank. In the Hebrew-Christian faith the body is a part of the whole man and is necessary for the completion of the total personality. It is, furthermore, necessary to the outward manifestation of the inner, spiritual reality. When we say, however, that man is made in the image of God we do not mean that he looks like God but that he is like him in his spiritual capacities—the power of thought, the power of communication, the power of choice, the power of self-transcendence.

2. *God Made Man Responsive*

This, we believe, is vital in God's creative purpose. He made man with capacities to respond. Not only can he respond with his animal senses—taste, touch, sight, sound, smell, which make him alive to his physical world and wonderfully so. Man possesses powers of the mind—reason, memory, imagination—that put him in touch with another world. He knows, and knows that he knows. He possesses emotional capacities. He can love, sympathize, laugh, know gratitude. Yet, there is still another dimension. He has the capacity to worship. He can believe, trust, hope. He knows he is more than animal. He is akin to one greater than himself. In some strange way he knows he is made for God. He can respond to God.

It is a great moment when a parent looks for the first time upon his child—lying there in that tiny bundle of flesh are all the capacities yet to be. It is an incomparably great moment when those powers awakened reach out in responsive love. The child not only knows it is a child but also knows its father—or mother.

Man possesses also the power of discrimination. He is a moral creature. He has the capacity to know good from evil —he can respond to both. He is granted the awesome power of the will to make his own choice. He can say no or he can say yes to God!

3. *God Made Man Responsible*

If man is to have the power to know, to feel, to will— that is, the capacity to respond—it then follows that he must be responsible for his actions.

"James Boswell in his memorable biography of Dr. Samuel Johnson tells us that Johnson spent all his days under the shadow of one stupendous text which hung over him like a daily judgment. This was the text: 'Unto whomsoever much is given, of him shall be much required.' Every thoughtful, decent person feels himself judged by that statement of our Lord. Like Doctor Johnson he feels responsive to what has been given him and he feels responsible for what is required of him. In order to make good in life, we must be both responsive and responsible." [3]

Man has been endowed by his creator with great powers. With that there comes very great responsibility.

First of all, he is responsible to the God who made him

and whose image he bears. This is the first and greatest of the commandments establishing man's relationship to his maker. "I am the Lord thy God, ... Thou shalt have no other gods before me" (Ex. 20:2–3). With even greater clarity Jesus set forth the claims of God's priority on our total being: "Jesus said unto him, Thou shalt love the Lord thy God with all thy heart, and with all thy soul, and with all thy mind. This is the first and great commandment" (Matt. 22:37–38).

Second, if man is to have dominion over this earth, to be fruitful, to multiply, to replenish, to subdue, then he must be responsible for the use he makes of it. Nowhere is this earth turned over to man to do as he pleases. It belongs to God, and it is to be used for his glory and for his purpose. Over and over the Bible emphasizes that it is required of man that he be found faithful, that he give a good account of that which has been entrusted to him. This is the theology of stewardship.

Thus, it must always be remembered that man was not alone. From the very beginning he is set in a larger context. He was to be a member of a family, a nation, and, finally, human society. As such it is required that he be a responsible member. Cain was Abel's brother; that he could not deny. That he should have been his brother's keeper was what God expected of him—and us. To deny this responsibility goes counter to one of the basic laws of life. Jesus said, "Thou shalt love thy neighbour as thyself" (Matt. 22:39).

Man, to have the privilege of living, under God, as overseer of the things of this earth and as a member of the family of mankind must be responsible.

4. *God Made Man Immortal*

One thing more must be said about the man God made. He was not only made for time. He was not only set in the larger context of human society. He was made for eternity. This is a further mark of his spiritual kinship with God. It is not our purpose here to go into the proof of man's existence beyond death, if indeed, it could be proved—as some ask for proof. It is to point out that God's eternal purpose for himself or for man cannot be fulfilled in one lifetime or one generation or the whole span of history. It can only be fulfilled in eternity. What man is and does here is set against that eternal background.

Man is never at home on this earth; he longs for another country; he rebels against the finality of time and death. He is made for eternity.

III. THE BROKEN IMAGE

If man had lived from the beginning and had continued to live on the level that God intended, he would have fulfilled God's purpose in creation. But tragically, man turned away from obedience to God to follow his own rebellious impulses. As a result, the image of God in him was broken. The plan was spoiled—though not defeated.

1. *The Problem of Evil*

The problem of evil and its entrance into the world must remain a baffling and unsolved mystery. The fact of its existence and the tragic consequences is undeniable. Everything that it touches it blights and ruins. Man's history had scarcely begun before he lost the paradise which God had given him. It caused his brother's blood to stain the good earth and robbed him of his unbroken fellowship with God.

Some years ago we visited the great Carlsbad Caverns in New Mexico. As we stood at the entrance waiting to be shown through, the guide said: "We ask you, please, not to touch the beautiful crystal formations. We have discovered that there is a chemical in the oil on the human hand that will discolor the formations. What God has taken millions of years to make beautiful," he continued, "man can make ugly in a moment!" Indeed, he can. There is evil in him that mars the image.

2. *The Confidence of God*

The confidence God had in his own creation was clearly shown in the fact that he made us free. Why did he so make us? It seems that the alternative would have been managed like a puppet on a string. He could not have sinned nor could he have loved. But man can sin and he can love. That is the danger and the glory of freedom. Each time we bring a child into the world we face that risk. If it grows to know, to see, to choose, then one day it may break our heart and destroy its own life. It also may stand tall and clean and fine and speak to us of its gratitude and devotion. Without the risk there could have been no sin, no greatness.

3. *The Riddle of the Universe*

"A Greek story tells how outside the city of Thebes there sat a monster called the Sphinx. To every passer-by she put a riddle: What creature has two feet, three feet, and four feet, and is weakest when it has most feet? Those who failed to solve the riddle she destroyed. The menace was eventually removed by Oedipus, who answered that it is a man who crawls on all fours as a baby, then walks upright on two feet, and finally moves only with the aid of a stick.

"It is becoming more and more apparent that the world we live in is a Sphinx. She propounds for us a riddle, and she will destroy us if we cannot solve it. But in this case man is not the answer: man is himself the riddle. What is this strange creature, half angel and half beast, capable alike of the heights of virtue and of the depths of depravity, who can control the forces of nature but not the passions of his own wayward heart? What is the meaning of the universe which has given him birth, but where he can never feel quite at home? What is the purpose of his brief, troubled, yet often majestic life? How is he to live at peace with his neighbors in a world which is rapidly becoming a single neighborhood? And how is he to live at peace with himself when his own soul is the battleground of warring emotions?" [4]

These are questions which now confront us. What will God do with the broken image? What will happen to his plan? How will man be made to fit into it? The plan was marred; it was not, it could not be, defeated.

IV. THE UNFOLDING PURPOSE

We have sketched, briefly, the beginning of God's creative work. We looked at man, the crown and goal of his creation— and then, this broken image. But God's purpose will not be defeated. In the long process of redemption the image could be restored, the plan fulfilled. In truth, it can be said. "If we have faith in our divine Creator," then, "there is coherence in the whole fabric of existence, and an unfolding purpose in history and in life. For a holy will created it, and supreme intention holds within itself the one far-off divine event, to which the whole creation moves." [5] Across the long stretches of history we watch that purpose unfold.

1. God's Purpose in Hebrew History

God's redemptive purpose begins to take shape, so far as Hebrew history is concerned, with a man. "Out of Ur of the Chaldeans, from among the miscellaneous and now-forgotten crowd, comes Abraham to be the pioneer of a new civilization of the spirit." [6] To him was given the promise and the redemptive commission. "Now the Lord had said unto Abram, Get thee out of thy country, and from thy kindred, and from thy father's house, unto a land that I will shew thee: and I will make of thee a great nation, and I will bless thee, and make thy name great; and thou shalt be a blessing: and I will bless them that bless thee, and curse him that curseth thee: and in thee shall all families of the earth be blessed" (Gen. 12:1–3). From there followed the formation of the lineage through which God would move—Isaac and Jacob, Judah and Joseph.

Then came the bondage of Israel in Egypt. From among those slaves God raised up his man Moses. Moses, the mighty giver of the law, would be God's instrument for the fashioning out of this slave people a great nation—a people which at their best would not forget that they were created for God's purpose. When they did forget—and they did—God called a man to light again the prophetic torch on the long road winding toward the fulfilment of destiny—Elijah and Elisha, Amos and Isaiah, Hosea and Jeremiah.

2. *God's Purpose in All History*

This was true not only of Bible history. It was true of all history. Although he was neither known nor named by some nations, God did not abdicate his sovereign right in the life of any nation. He turned the exploits of pagan people to serve his purpose—Persia and Egypt, Babylon and Rome. Listen, for instance, to his word to the Persian king, Cyrus: "Thus saith the Lord to his anointed, to Cyrus, whose right I have holden, to subdue nations before him; . . . For Jacob my servant's sake, and Israel mine elect, I have even called thee by thy name: . . . I am the Lord, and there is none else, there is no God beside me" (Isa. 45:1–5).

It is with this same insight that Victor Hugo writes in *Les Miserables*. "He was writing of the Battle of Waterloo and the defeat of Napoleon, a defeat which might have seemed to have its immediate explanation in the fact that the reinforcements which might have saved him were misdirected, and did not arrive in time—or in Hugo's words, 'Because on the afternoon of a certain summer's day, a shepherd said to a Prussian in the forest, "Go this way and not that." ' But the real cause as Victor Hugo saw it, was more majestic.

'End of the dictatorship. A whole European system crumbled away. . . .

'Was it possible that Napoleon should have won that battle? We answer No. Why? Because of Wellington? Because of Blucher? No. Because of God. . . .

"Napoleon had been denounced in the infinite, and his fall had been decided on.

'He embarrassed God.

'Waterloo is not a battle; it is a change of front on the part of the Universe.' " [7] No nation or man is exempt from God's inexorable purpose.

3. *God's Purpose in Making Man*

Always at the center of God's purpose is a man. That is one of the marvels of God's way. He deals in vast expanses of time and history, but he never leaves out the individual. He works through a Noah or an Abraham or a David.

"Moses would never have led the Exodus unless the spirit of God had first laid hold of him in the vision of the burning bush and challenged and corrected him and compelled him to conquer his own self-distrust. Hosea became the passionate prophet of the love of God because he learned through his suffering. The revolution wrought in Saul of Tarsus, the conversion of Augustine, the transformation of the careless Francis of Assisi into the saint—all these are examples of the way God creates something different out of what seemed to be of a fixed mold. Added to those are the uncounted instances, familiar to every generation, of persons who at first seemed altogether ordinary, but who by steady obedience to the moving of the Spirit became great servants of God." [8]

4. *God's Purpose Fulfilled in Christ*

Slowly but steadily God moves forward through his redemptive purpose toward his goal in history—the creation of a new humanity by the making of a new man.

That is to be accomplished through his Son Jesus Christ. It was in Christ that God purposed our redemption from the foundation of the world. He came to make known that purpose unto us. He came, lived, died and was raised from the dead that man might become in him a new creation. "God was in Christ, reconciling the world unto himself" (2 Cor. 5:19).

So Paul gives to Christ the place of pre-eminence in all God's redemptive purpose. "He is the image of the invisible God, the first-born of all creation; for in him all things were created, in heaven and on earth, visible and invisible, whether thrones or dominions or principalities or authorities—all things were created through him and for him. He is before all things, and in him all things hold together. He is the head of the body, the church; he is the beginning, the first-born from the dead, that in everything he might be pre-eminent. For in him all the fulness of God was pleased to dwell, and through him to reconcile to himself all things, whether on earth or in heaven, making peace by the blood of his cross" (Col. 1:15–20, RSV).

Concerning the end which God had in mind from the beginning, E. Y. Mullins says it was "to produce a kingdom in which his own image should be reflected, in which his own glory should appear. The end thus defined was an end begun, carried forward, and to be completed in Jesus Christ." [9]

FOR FURTHER STUDY AND DISCUSSION

1. Discuss the evidences all about us that there is a purpose back of this created universe.
2. Discuss the various views held concerning men—the communist, the materialist, the evolutionist, the Christian.
3. Did God know that man was going to sin and spoil his purpose; if so, why did he make him as he did?
4. From the story of the Bible and from the evidence in history and in life—your own if you like—discuss the evidences of God's unfolding purpose.

CHAPTER 2 OUTLINE

I. GOD'S PART IN THE NEW CREATION

   1. The Father and the Redemptive Purpose

   2. Jesus Christ and the Redemptive Act

   3. The Holy Spirit and the Redemptive Experience

II. WHEN MAN MEETS GOD'S TERMS

   1. What a Man Must Know

   2. What a Man Must Do

   3. What a Man Must Believe

III. THE EXPERIENCE OF THE NEW BIRTH

   1. Many Terms but One Meaning

   2. A Variety of Experiences but One Experience

   3. The Meaning of the New Birth

2

The Great Encounter—
the New Life in Christ

THE JOURNEY of a thousand miles begins with the first step. If there is not that first step—taken in the right direction—the goal will never be attained. Beginnings are of great importance. Whatever we hope to finish we will do well to make the right start—a race, a job, a marriage, or a life!

So far as the Christian life is concerned, it is not only important, it is absolutely essential. Indeed, if it does not begin right it never begins at all.

The Christian life begins with a definite encounter with Jesus Christ and results in a new creation. Paul thus describes the experience: "Therefore if any man be in Christ, he is a new creature: old things are passed away; behold, all things are become new" (2 Cor. 5:17). We set ourselves now to try to understand that experience—to make the right beginning in the new life in Christ.

What makes Christianity a gospel is its affirmation that neither man nor society need stay the way they are. Human nature can be changed. Alongside of education and legislation it sets another watchword, its distinctive watchword—regeneration. If Christianity affirms anything at all, it is that human nature can be changed, genuinely, radically, and permanently changed.

We face this frightful new age knowing we must have new men. We know further that in the gospel of Jesus Christ we have the power to make that dream come true.

I. God's Part in the New Creation

On the ceiling of the Sistine Chapel in Rome is one of Michelangelo's frescoes depicting the creation of Adam. The first man is lying, perfect in his human form, but listless and without animation. Above him is the figure of God coming down as out of heaven in a great wind with his arm stretched out and his finger touching the limp finger of Adam that he might catch the spark of life. Without God he could not become a living soul.

As it was in the creation at the beginning so is God's work in the recreation of new life. Man that was dead in trespasses and sin becomes a new creature and begins a new state of existence.

God's purpose is one complete and continuous work of grace. It was initiated by God; it was made possible through Jesus Christ; it is brought to man by his Holy Spirit. Let us look more closely at the part each plays.

1. The Father and the Redemptive Purpose

The plan for the new creation—for man's redemption—had its beginning with God. Out of his creative love he has made us; by his creative love he would save us (John 3:16). There could be no greater foundation for our hope and assurance than that. Our redemption does not depend upon us but upon him who made and purposed our salvation from the start.

Dr. Conner says, "Not only did God work to bring us to himself; he worked in pursuance of a plan that is eternal. He did not suddenly decide to work for a certain man's salvation; he worked for the man's salvation because he purposed to do so from eternal ages." [1]

So, too, does Paul understand the eternal purpose of God. Writing to the Ephesians he says, "Blessed be the God and Father of our Lord Jesus Christ, who has blessed us in Christ with every spiritual blessing in the heavenly places, even as he chose us in him before the foundation of the world, that we should be holy and blameless before him. He destined us in love to be his sons through Jesus Christ, according to the purpose of his will, to the praise of his glorious grace which he freely bestowed on us in the Beloved" (Eph. 1:3–6, RSV). We believe that that purpose applies not only to all men but to each man.

God's purpose is inclusive not exclusive. He wills to save all who will be saved. The fact must be made clear that the saving miracle is with God. Man, the sinner, is utterly dependent upon God for his regeneration. God makes the provision; God prescribes the condition; God makes the approach; God quickens the flagging spirit of man to response. Without God man can do nothing. He must be born from above!

2. *Jesus Christ and the Redemptive Act*

Volumes have been and could be written on the life and work of Jesus Christ. He is inexhaustible in his revelation. He reveals the truth about God. "He that hath seen me hath seen the Father" (John 14:9). He tells the truth about life. "In him was life, and the life was the light of men. The true light that enlightens every man was coming into the world" (John 1:4, 9, RSV). He came and lived the life that man might know what life was meant to be and how it was to be lived. Indeed, his claim for himself could be said of no other who ever lived. "Jesus saith unto him, I am the way, the truth, and the life: no man cometh unto the Father, but by me" (John 14:6).

The chief reason for his coming, however, was redemptive. We have it in his own words. "The Son of man is come to seek and to save that which was lost" (Luke 19:10). This is the story of the Bible. It runs through it like a river of living water reaching its crest in the saving act of Christ on the cross. In one sweeping statement Paul sets forth this mighty act of God. "God was in Christ, reconciling the world unto himself" (2 Cor. 5:19). In Christ, because of who he was, the Son of God and the Son of man, God was at work redeeming man. In his death on the cross, voluntarily accepted by Christ, he was giving himself for man's salvation. On the cross God's righteousness was being vindicated and the demands of the moral law fulfilled. There he was winning the victory over sin.

On the cross we see God's love in action. "But God commendeth his love toward us, in that, while we were yet sinners, Christ died for us" (Rom. 5:8). "It was love going to the limit of suffering and agony to redeem the lost from the ruin of their own sin. The cross of Christ is the pledge of God's love for a sinful and ruined race. As such the cross represents an act of grace. It stands for God's gracious love going out to redeem man as sinful and unworthy." [2]

The resurrection was God's approval that the victory had been won. Christ had met man's enemy in mortal combat. Sin had done its worst and it was not enough. In Christ the broken relationship had been bridged, the broken image could be restored, the old life could be made new. This incomparable event cannot be reduced to a mechanical formula; it cannot be explained by theories. It beggars our finite mind. We can only stand amazed in his presence on Calvary and try to grasp what God was doing there in Christ. For "there God grappled with our sin in the cleansing tragedy of holiness: 'For our sake he made him to be sin who knew no sin.' There God gathered all the spears of man's transgression into his own breast. They were small-part actors in a drama too vast for their comprehension. Heaven met the power of evil in dread encounter on Calvary, and conquered in love's seeming defeat." [3]

We do know that there on that hill God's holy will and suffering love were forgiving our sins and making possible our new life in Christ. For there "He has delivered us from the dominion of darkness and transferred us to the kingdom of his beloved Son, in whom we have redemption, the forgiveness of sins" (Col. 1:13-14, RSV).

3. *The Holy Spirit and the Redemptive Experience*

The Holy Spirit carries the purpose of God, perfected through his Son Jesus Christ, into the experience of man. So the gospel message is a continuing story. What Christ did the Holy Spirit will continue to carry to the very citadel of man's heart.

Luke brings his gospel to a close by saying, "Thus it is written, and thus it behoved Christ to suffer, and to rise from the dead the third day: and that repentance and remission of sins should be preached in his name among all nations, beginning at Jerusalem" (Luke 24:46-47). He opens the book of Acts with these words: "The former treatise have I made, O Theophilus, of all that Jesus began both to do and teach, until the day in which he was taken up, after that he through the Holy Ghost had given commandments unto the apostles whom he had chosen" (Acts 1:1-2).

The two are identified in God's redemptive work. "As victor over sin and death, Christ sends the Spirit on his people. He shed forth the Spirit on the day of Pentecost (Acts 2:33). He is now the living, super-historical Christ. As such he sheds forth his Spirit on his people. And the work of the Spirit is to make him Saviour and Lord in the lives of men. . . . The Spirit's presence is the presence of Christ. Pentecost was the extension in the lives of men of the redemptive power of the death and the resurrection of Jesus." [4]

So God is at work through the Holy Spirit bringing the gospel of Christ into man's experience. He carries the message to our hearts. He circles our lives seeking to find a landing place. As compassionately as Christ seeks the lost so he seeks a way of entrance into our inner experience. Jesus thus describes his activity. "And when he comes, he will convince the world of sin and of righteousness and of judgment: of sin, because they do not believe in me; of righteousness, because I go to the Father, and you will see me no more; of judgment, because the ruler of this world is judged" (John 16:8–11, RSV). He opens our eyes to the awfulness of sin. He confronts us with the reality of Christ. He presents us with the choice that is like a final judgment—as indeed, it is—for or against.

When once we open to him our life, he effects the miracle of the new birth. One Bible scholar says: "What Christ has wrought in his redemptive life and death and resurrection becomes real to us through the Spirit. The atonement of Christ is sufficient for all, but it becomes efficient for the individual only as he yields to the Spirit. . . . Only then will we have his power, and grace, and love." [5] God has left nothing undone to make possible for us the new life. It remains for us to accept it on his terms.

II. When Man Meets God's Terms

We stand now at the crossroads, and man must choose. God has purposed his redemption and in Jesus Christ has provided for it. His Spirit is beaconing us. If we are to begin the new life we must respond. We cannot draw a line and say, "God comes this far and no farther." The demarcation between God's part and man's is not so clearly defined. Man cannot enter into the new life except for what God has done for him. He will not enter in unless his response is quickened by the Holy Spirit. God in his infinite love and grace takes the initiative always, but man must respond. It is a mutual experience.

Conversion begins, unfolds, is consummated in the realm of the human spirit. In describing it we use certain words—conviction, repentance, faith, confession. But these are not merely steps in a mechanically conceived plan. Nor are they separated into compartments. They are elements in a total experience involving the whole personality of man. It does not result in just part of a man—his mind or emotions—becoming new. The end result is a new being.

1. *What a Man Must Know*

It goes without saying, if a man is to become a Christian he must know about Jesus Christ and the truth of his gospel. But this we cannot take for granted. God is conceived in many ways—from "Mobile Cosmic Ether" to "The Man Upstairs." God uses many means to reveal himself to man, but man's knowledge of Christ has its source in God's Word. There we find the story of the historical Christ and through that medium comes the voice of the Living Word.

Jesus' call to repentance and faith came only as he confronted men with himself and the gospel of his kingdom (Mark 1:14-15). John gives us the purpose for writing his gospel by saying, "But these are written, that ye might believe that Jesus is the Christ, the Son of God; and that believing ye might have life through his name" (John 20:31). Paul reminds us: "Whosoever shall call upon the name of the Lord shall be saved. How then shall they call on him in whom they have not believed? and how shall they believe in him of whom they have not heard?" (Rom. 10:13-14).

The Christian life cannot begin, therefore, without a knowledge of, and encounter with, Jesus Christ.

2. *What a Man Must Do*

In the experience of becoming a Christian there must be a turning—a turning from sin to God. There must be a change of mind, a change in the object of love, a change in the course of the will, a changed center of life. The word is repentance. When one asks the question, "What must I do to be saved?" the first word is "repent."

What does that mean in terms of experience? It is a change

involving the total personality. As Dr. Mullins says, "The word repentance is the translation of two Greek words in the New Testament. One of these is *metamelomai*. This word expresses the emotional element in repentance. It means regret. But this regret may be of a godly sort leading to genuine repentance, or it may be a regret which produces no moral change. The other New Testament word translated repentance is *metanoia*. This word means a change of the mind or thought. But the change of mind expressed by this word is more than a mere intellectual change of view. It carries with it the idea of will. It is clear, then, that man's spiritual nature as a whole acts when he repents. It is not one faculty or function of the soul, but his entire spirit."

It means a change of mind. He begins to think of sin, of God, of others, of life in a different way.

It involves a change of feeling or emotions. What he once loved he no longer loves. A new object of devotion has moved in as the controlling center of his life. It means, also, a voluntary changing of the will. His life is set in a new direction. God's purpose and God's will become his accepted and habitual way of life.

Repentance is not simply an inward experience. When genuine it manifests itself in the way we live. This was the kind of repentance John the Baptist was calling for. "Bear fruit that befits repentance, and do not presume to say to yourselves, 'We have Abraham as our father'; for I tell you, God is able from these stones to raise up children to Abraham" (Matt. 3:8-9, RSV). It calls for our confession with our lips, but it calls even more insistently for our confession with our daily living.

So daring and so demanding is repentance that man does not have the resources within himself to exercise it. It, too, calls for help from the Spirit. It demands that our faith in God stand beside it.

3. *What a Man Must Believe*

Faith occupies a central place in life. We cannot live without faith. Robert Louis Stevenson was right when he said that faith forms the axles of the universe. Faith is the working principle of daily living, manifested in the tiny tot crossing the street with her hand in the hand of her mother. Faith is manifested in a Columbus crossing the Atlantic when his only chart was one "which faith deciphered in the skies."

Here, however, we are concerned with the faith that brings us into a redeeming experience with Jesus Christ. It stands beside the experience of repentance as man's response to the gospel. Faith and repentance are inseparable in this experience. In the New Testament sometimes repentance stands alone (Luke 13:3). In other places faith stands alone (Acts 16:31). Still in others they stand together (Acts 20:21). But they are part of the one experience.

There is common agreement that if this experience is to lead to conversion there must be in it these three elements. There is the intellectual element. We must believe that God is. We must believe in the reality of Jesus Christ and what he did for us. It is not enough, however, for us to accept this as an historical fact or agree with it as a Christian dogma. There is the element of personal faith. Christ did this for me. I am involved in his death, his resurrection. "I am crucified with Christ": Paul said, "nevertheless I live; yet not I, but Christ liveth in me: and the life which I now live in the flesh I live by the faith of the Son of God, who loved me, and gave himself for me" (Gal. 2:20).

If we go this far we must go all the way. We must stake our life on that truth. We must make the venture, committing our life to Jesus Christ as Saviour and Lord, now and forever. This is the faith that makes Christ the living center of our life. This is the faith that saves and makes new. We open the door, he does the rest. But the opening of the door is our decision. Only those who have made the venture know how unfailingly true it is.

III. THE EXPERIENCE OF THE NEW BIRTH

In this chapter we have endeavored to trace the steps leading up to the encounter between God and man that results in the new creation. This world—old or new—demands a new man. There is no hope either for the world or man short of that. And it was a new man that God purposed to create through Jesus Christ. Man cannot be self-made. Only in Christ can he become a new creature. Christianity stands or falls on that claim.

By whatever name we call the experience of the new creation as Edwin Markham says, "Christ's miracle was to make a Christian from our common clay."

1. *Many Terms but One Meaning*

Many terms are used to describe this experience of our becoming a new creation. Sometimes it is a word or group of words—regeneration, the new birth, adoption, conversion, or a new creature. Sometimes the experience is clothed in word pictures. Like the prodigal son: "This my son was dead, and is alive again; he was lost, and is found" (Luke 15:24). Paul speaks of turning "from darkness to light" (Acts 26:18), John, of passing "from death unto life" (1 John 3:14). But all of these words and figures of speech are different ways of describing the making of a new man. There are shades of difference, to be sure, but the end result is the same.

2. *A Variety of Experiences but One Experience*

We must keep in mind, also, that in this experience there is room for vast variety. We may too often try to interpret the validity of everyone's experience in terms of our own or insist that theirs be identical with ours.

Paul's, indeed, was sudden and cataclysmic. But Matthew quietly left his place of business and followed Jesus. Mary Magdalene may have had to undergo deep spiritual surgery to become a new person. A little child possesses the quality and spirit to become a child of the Master's kingdom without these unusual experiences, for he has not become hardened or resentful.

One has only to think of the variety of Christian experiences in the Bible and out of it to know how true this is. They are men out of the far past or the immediate present—Augustine and Luther, John Wesley and George Whitefield, Charles H. Spurgeon and Dwight L. Moody, C. S. Lewis and Billy Graham. The light broke upon each in a different way, and yet they came from their encounter with Christ new and changed men. So the new life must begin for each one of us or there is no beginning.

3. *The Meaning of the New Birth*

Says Paul Tillich, "If I were asked to sum up the Christian message for our time in two words, I would say with Paul: It is the message of a 'New Creation.' We have read something of the New Creation in Paul's second letter to the Corinthians. Let me repeat one of his sentences in the words of an exact translation: 'If anyone is in union with Christ he is a new being; the old state of things has passed away; there is a new state of things.' Christianity is the message of the New Creation, the New Being." [6]

Just how this "old" creature becomes "new" shall ever remain a mystery. That is the problem with which Nicodemus wrestled the night Jesus talked with him. And even in Jesus' strikingly simple explanation the mystery abides. It is like a new birth, a birth from above, a spiritual birth, he said. Or again, it is like the wind. "The wind bloweth where it listeth, and thou hearest the sound thereof, but canst not tell whence it cometh, and whither it goeth: so is every one that is born of the Spirit" (John 3:8). It still remains a mystery, but we know and we see the change that it makes.

God touches the old life by his Spirit, and man responds in repenting, trusting faith, and the miracle happens. Citron describes it like this: "The relationship between creation and re-creation is a real one, but as any two things which are similar are not identical, so are the first and the second creation two different acts of God. The material used by God in his workshop as he forms the new man, is not 'the dust of the earth' nor a stone or a stock, but humanity. The great change does not mean that some lifeless matter is transformed into a human personality, nor does it imply that the natural man is raised to the estate of an angel or a superman. Man is man. By his regeneration he becomes a Christian." [7]

In answer to the question, "What is this New Being?" Tillich says, "The New Being is not something that simply takes the place of the Old Being. But it is a renewal of the old which has been corrupted, distorted, split and almost destroyed. But not wholly destroyed. Salvation does not destroy creation; but it transforms the old creation into a new one." [8] And, most vividly of all, by man's personal involvement in Christ's death and resurrection, the "old" is crucified with Christ, the old nature dies and the "new" is raised to the newness of life (Rom. 6:5–8, RSV).

This then is the beginning of the new life. It comes from God. It is accepted by man on God's terms. The new birth brings a radical change in the aim and purpose of life. Man comes into possession of a new set of motives and a moral and spiritual renewal of the will. The change can only be described as the "New Creation." It is the beginning, as we shall see, of a lifelong experience.

FOR FURTHER STUDY AND DISCUSSION

1. Discuss some of the Utopias—dreams of perfect societies that man has tried to build and the causes of their subsequent failures.
2. Discuss the distinctive part that each member of the Godhead has in man's regeneration—the Father, the Son, the Holy Spirit.
3. Discuss ways by which we can lead those who are not Christians to more fully understand the vital elements in the experience of regeneration—repentance, faith, confession.
4. There is a wide variety in the experience of regeneration. Take time to relate individual conversion experiences to verify this fact.

CHAPTER 3 OUTLINE

I. SALVATION—A CONTINUING LIFE

    1. Salvation Is a Definite Experience

    2. Salvation Is a Lifetime Experience

    3. Salvation Is a Consummation

II. THE CONTINUING STRUGGLE

    1. The Uphill Road

    2. The Enemy

    3. The Enemy from Without

    4. The Response from Within

III. THE DEMANDS OF DISCIPLESHIP

    1. The Call to Discipleship

    2. Christ and His Cross

    3. The Christian and His Cross

3

The Continuing Struggle—
the New Warfare

IN LIFE'S HIGHEST ACHIEVEMENTS we stand not at the end but at the beginning. How often, for instance, do our stories end with the goal of marriage—"and they lived happily ever after." To be sure, marriage is an achievement, but it is only the beginning of what can be a life that is rich and full beyond anything we have ever known before.

The same is true of the birth of a baby. With what planning and ever-growing expectancy parents wait for the arrival of their child. Then, at last, it arrives. The long-expected event is a joyous reality. But who has not looked at the object of all that excitement and felt not the "end of something" but the "beginning." The span of a whole lifetime unfolds before this new life.

I. Salvation—a Continuing Life

So it is with our experience of becoming a Christian. There is no experience that is so far reaching, so life changing. Life moves forward and backward to that experience. We lay great importance upon the necessity of the new birth, and rightly so. However, this great achievement is not the end—either for the one who has had the experience or those of us responsible for him.

We must come to see that the Christian life is a continuing life. It covers the whole span of a lifetime—and beyond. There is a biblical, a theological basis for such a view. At this point Dr. W. T. Conner asks some thought-provoking questions. "Is salvation something that takes place all at once or is it a continuous process? In approaching the matter, it will help us to keep in mind that salvation is an act, a process, and a consummation. We might put the matter in the form of a question. Is a Christian saved, is he being saved, or is he to be saved in the future? It is made abundantly clear in the New Testament that he is all three—saved, being saved, and going to be saved." [1]

1. *Salvation Is a Definite Experience*

If this initial experience is insincere or never becomes a genuine reality then the whole attempt at living the Christian life is built upon a foundation that cannot, by its very nature, endure. There *must* be a right beginning. That involves a definite decision for Christ, a divine-human encounter that results in a new creation.

Regeneration is an act of God rather than a human achievement. It is true that man must meet the conditions, but man cannot effect the change. He is born from above. We believe that the act itself is instantaneous. That which sometimes makes it appear to be gradual is the slowness with which man comes to the point of surrender and acceptance. He may come gradually to the point of breaking with sin and trusting in Christ, but once he repents and believes, God is ready to accomplish his work of regeneration. Or to put it another way: "I think every conversion, if it be true, has in it elements of crisis and of process. Our exposure to Christian dynamic may take some time; it is gradual. Our final decision about Christ must be, like all decisions, conscious and instantaneous." [2]

Paul's own experience is the classic example. That he was under deep conviction for some time seems quite certain. When Christ stepped in, the turning was dramatic and definite. In speaking of that experience—his and ours—he said, "By grace you have been saved through faith; and this is not your own doing, it is the gift of God—" (Eph. 2:8, RSV).

Or again, "Therefore, since we are justified by faith, we have peace with God through our Lord Jesus Christ" (Rom. 5:1, RSV). The tense of the Greek verbs in these passages speaks with a kind of finality. The action is not continuous; it is completed.

Salvation, then, is definite; it has a beginning. It is like getting on a ship. We move quickly from where we used to be. We have not yet arrived at our ultimate destination—of course not! That will take time and travel. But we have begun the journey.

2. *Salvation Is a Lifetime Experience*

This is an exceedingly important phase of our being saved that we have not always made clear. Indeed, I wonder if we in some measure are not responsible for that alarming number of people who hold membership in our churches but whose lives mean little or nothing to Christ—nor he to them. We have preached, all too glibly, the doctrine "once saved, always saved" without being too careful to explain all that is involved—if we knew! People have "come forward" at our invitation, "filled out the card," were "received into the church" and "baptized." They did all we asked them to do. When they realized that they were saved, nothing else seemed to matter too much. If they didn't reason that out, at least half of the members of our churches are "living it out"! Salvation for them is not a continuing experience. Next to the tragedy of not being saved at all is the tragedy of arrested spiritual development.

The pattern of the New Testament is different. Luke says concerning the experience at Pentecost: "Then they that gladly received his word were baptized: and the same day there were added unto them about three thousand souls. And they *continued* stedfastly in the apostles' doctrine and fellowship, and in breaking of bread, and in prayers" (Acts 2:41–42).

The same grace by which a man is saved in the beginning continues to stand by him in his effort to live out his salvation in each day's experience. Paul says, "Through him we have obtained access to this grace in which we stand, and we rejoice in our hope of sharing the glory of God. More than that, we rejoice in our sufferings, knowing that suffering produces endurance, and endurance produces character, and character produces hope, and hope does not disappoint us, because God's love has been poured into our hearts through the Holy Spirit which has been given to us" (Rom. 5:2–5, RSV). This is the autobiography of his unfolding Christian experience.

The cross of Christ is not only central in a man becoming a new creation; it is central in a man living a growing, creative Christian life. It is for them, too, the power of God. "The word of the cross is folly to those who are perishing, but to us who are being saved it is the power of God" (1 Cor. 1:18, RSV). Paul is speaking here of the continuing salvation.

God's purpose then is not just to "save a soul"; it is to save a life—a whole life for a whole lifetime—and eternity. "The spiritual life is union with God in love, leading ultimately to reconciliation, wholeness, and unity. It is both a gift and a task: a gift, which keeps us utterly dependent upon God, and a task, which we must pursue with unremitting earnestness and resolution to the last day of our lives." [3] These two ideas are also present in Paul's word, "Work out your own salvation with fear and trembling; for God is at work in you, both to will and to work for his good pleasure" (Phil. 2:12–13, RSV).

Says Dr. Mullins, "The aim of God in establishing his kingdom among men is to produce holy men and women, both as individuals in their relations to him and as members of a holy society. In the accomplishment of this aim, two things are necessary: first, the establishment of a new relation between God and men, and secondly, the production of a new character corresponding to the new relation." [4]

3. *Salvation Is a Consummation*

God does not start what he does not intend to finish. His purpose is to save us in the beginning, along the way, and at the end of the journey. That is our hope and security. Who could better have understood this from his own experiences than the apostle Peter. Writing in his first letter he says, "Blessed be the God and Father of our Lord Jesus Christ! By his great mercy we have been born anew to a living hope through the resurrection of Jesus Christ from the dead, and to an inheritance which is imperishable, undefiled, and unfading, kept in heaven for you, who by God's power are guarded through faith for a salvation ready to be revealed in the last time (1 Peter 1:3–7, RSV). His faith covers the whole range of a man's existence. His security is in God's power to keep—and God's grace to enable him to endure in the process of refinement.

For Paul there never was a stopping place. He thinks of both creation and man as living in expectancy of the final consummation of our hope in Christ. "For the creation waits with eager longing for the revealing of the sons of God; for the creation was subjected to futility, not of its own will but by the will of him who subjected it in hope; because the creation itself will be set free from its bondage to decay and obtain the glorious liberty of the children of God. We know that the whole creation has been groaning in travail together until now; and not only the creation, but we ourselves, who have the first fruits of the Spirit, groan inwardly as we wait for adoption as sons, the redemption of our bodies" (Rom. 8:19–23, RSV).

Yes, salvation is a continuing experience; it is a lifetime, it is for eternity. Our doctrine of "the perseverance of the saints" is not ill-founded. We do not claim to know all. It certainly invites continuous study. But let us not sell it short. If our encounter in the beginning is genuine, if we are born to a new life, God will see us through.

II. THE CONTINUING STRUGGLE

There is the greatest shock in store for the new Christian who begins his journey with the impression that now that he is a Christian all of his problems are over. As we shall see, Christ not only leads us out of trouble; he also leads us into trouble.

1. *The Uphill Road*

It is far better to know at the beginning what we are in for. Every new Christian—indeed, every Christian—ought to take time to read John Bunyan's immortal allegory, *Pilgrim's Progress*. Its story is clothed in ancient and figurative language, but its insight into the nature of evil and man's struggle against sin is unsurpassed in any age or language apart from the Bible itself. "Here," says one "is a picture-map of the country through which we must expect to travel. First comes the region of beginnings—a wonderful place. It is a green and pleasant land, full of the sights and sounds of springtime. This is the time of 'conversion' or of a new start. This is followed by a vast expanse of wilderness, with its own lights and shadows, but with much toiling through the shifting sand, or walking along narrow paths through dark and arid gorges—a time of hard going, broken only now and again by an open valley among the mountains, or by an oasis in the sandy desert. This region symbolizes a period in life which is full of difficulty, a time when we are even tempted to give up the journey and settle down at the next stopping-place, or even to lie down and die. This central wilderness is ten times the length of the first region.

"Then, when we have safely emerged from the perils of

the wilderness, we come to a region of high mountains, beautiful, well-watered, but rocky and very steep. The whole country is full of beauty and majesty, but it is also the scene of great storms, when everything is blotted out, and as we climb we can see nothing ahead but snow and ice, or rain and mist. This is a region of great joy as well as of great trial. But it does not matter where we are when death comes; all that does matter is that we are in the way, pressing forward all the time.

"This picture-map suggests two things: (a) that difficulties and temptations are only to be expected on this journey; they are part of a traveller's normal experience; (b) that this central wilderness is the longest and toughest part of the journey. It is like plodding through soft sand, with a warm wind in your face. It is monotonous and tiring; though the steady grind is relieved now and again by glimpses of beauty." [5]

It is a true picture. For the road leads uphill all the way. The Christian life began for me as I sat in the balcony of a great coliseum where the famed evangelist, Billy Sunday, was holding one of the last of his city-wide meetings. After my conversion I was given a little folder with a personal word from Mr. Sunday and a twofold message: (1) what it means to be a Christian and (2) how to make a success of the Christian life. Underneath was a sentence that proved to be both timely and prophetic, "Do not become discouraged. Expect temptations, discouragement, and persecution; *the Christian life is a warfare.*"

What are those forces that contend for our lives even after we have surrendered to Christ?

2. *The Enemy*

Man has been described as caught in the whirlpool of contending forces, himself the prize that is sought. On the one side is God in whose image man is made. On the other side is sin—that dark streak that runs across human nature, spoiling our best efforts, twisting our true nature out of shape, and, if possible, completely destroying us. And the father of sin is Satan.

We shall not here contend for ancient conceptions of his manifestation. His name may change; his appearance is much more apt to be in keeping with the latest fashion. He may at times succeed in getting the intellectual to believe he is nonexistent, or, at least he pours himself into psychological concepts and complexes! He has not, however, given up. With the modern *Rediscovery of Sin* and C. S. Lewis' *The Screwtape Letters* and more recently the insistent and almost unanimous warning of the nuclear scientists, he has once again taken his place as a respected contender for this world and the lives of men. Call him what you will; name sin by some other name, the dreadful reality of Eden and of Job and of the Wilderness of Temptation is with us today. He does not give up easily. He fought God's Son to death on a cross. He will contend for man's life, yes, even redeemed man's life all the way.

Paul gives us his dimensions in this penetrating analysis: "For we wrestle not against flesh and blood, but against principalities, against powers, against the rulers of the darkness of this world, against spiritual wickedness in high places" (Eph. 6:12). This, then, is the enemy we are up against. This is our spiritual warfare. We contend with forces that are more than human. We know the odds for winning are against us if we stand alone.

3. *The Enemy from Without*

The traditional, indeed the biblical, terms for man's age-old enemies are—the devil, the world, and the flesh.

What do we mean by "the world"? In the larger sense it is the cosmos, the whole created system. For us it is the world in which we live. The sum total of our environment. In the sense that it is identified with evil in the Bible it is that in our environment which appeals to us to do wrong. It is regarded as the arena in and through which evil forces operate.

The strategy of Satan in the Garden of Eden has changed. He uses God's good and endeavors to get man to pervert it to his own purposes. He promises man knowledge—"You shall be as gods." He promises man power—"The world is yours, use it as you please." He promises him approval—"Follow the lower standards and receive popular applause." He promises him superficial satisfaction—"Man does live by bread alone."

Let us make no mistake—evil still makes its bid through the world. The voice is claimant in our secular culture. It calls us to live apart from God, live independent of God, take what we can and use it or waste it. It makes us believe that life can be satisfied with things. "Build bigger barns," it says, "and bigger cities and bigger missiles." Then, "Take your ease, eat, drink, and be merry." What a mirage, what a colossal lie! That is the appeal of the world—without God.

4. *The Response from Within*

There is that within us that responds to the world about us. Just as there is that which responds to beauty and harmony and love so there is that which responds to evil. The Bible uses the word "flesh." Those ancients, as do we, felt the tug of unsatisfied appetites crying out to be fed.

What did they mean by the "flesh"? They did not mean that the physical was evil. God made that, too. By the flesh the New Testament means man's sinful nature or desires which find in the flesh their sphere of action. Here again evil takes God's good and perverts it for his purposes.

The world says, "Take me, use me for your own" and the pride of possession responds. The world says, "You can have your own way, be free"; the selfish ego within us takes over. The forbidden in the world says, "Taste me, use me to satisfy," and the hunger within us answers. The more often we respond the easier it becomes, the more deeply embedded the habit. Then when the Christian conscience says no to our bent to pride and selfishness and lust, the more bitter becomes the struggle.

This inner warfare the Bible describes as: "The desires of the flesh are against the Spirit, and the desires of the Spirit are against the flesh; for these are opposed to each other, to prevent you from doing what you would" (Gal. 5:17, RSV). If the desires of the flesh are allowed to take over we reap the terrible harvest of sin. "Each person is tempted when he is lured and enticed by his own desire. Then desire when it has conceived gives birth to sin; and sin when it is full-grown brings forth death" (James 1:14-15, RSV).

So each man, like Bunyan's pilgrim, travels "the way" from the gate of life to that distant goal. Powers of darkness beyond his knowing lurk in the shadows, the world offers its enticement, and hungers within him rise up to be satisfied. The struggle is on. It never lets up.

III. THE DEMANDS OF DISCIPLESHIP

Discipleship calls for a lifetime commitment. God in Christ has provided for the beginning, the way, the fulfilment. The way is not easy.

We have discussed the downward drag upon the Christian life by sin. The outward appeal of the world and the inward pull of our own sinful desires do indeed make the Christian life one of struggle. This moral struggle—the warfare between right and wrong—is one that goes on in all lives to one degree or another. There is, however, a struggle that is peculiar to the followers of Christ. It is not so much a struggle against the call of the low road as it is recoiling against the call of the high road. It is that within us that makes us unwilling to accept the discipline of the narrow way. To walk that way, however, is the high cost of Christian discipleship.

So does the Master challenge those who would follow

him: "Enter ye in at the strait gate: for wide is the gate, and broad is the way, that leadeth to destruction, and many there be which go in thereat: because strait is the gate, and narrow is the way, which leadeth unto life, and few there be that find it" (Matt. 7:13–14).

1. *The Call to Discipleship*

Jesus calls us to be his disciples—not just those who would serve him but all men. There are not two or three classifications for followers of Christ; there is one. We are to be "learners." We are to know the discipline of mind and spirit to give up "some things" that we may have "other things." We come to learn as little children, willing to learn—or else we cannot come at all. We grow toward Christian maturity by denying ourselves so that Christ may have his way in us.

The mark of any great leader is that he should state clearly the terms of his discipleship. Garibaldi offered his followers hunger and death—and Italy's freedom. King Arthur bound his knights "by so strait vows to his own self" that they were dazed as if "half-blinded at the coming of a light." No one could ever accuse Jesus of getting men to follow him under false pretenses. He told them plainly what they were in for. He knew what it would cost him—and them—to follow him. To those who enthusiastically volunteered to follow him wherever he should go, he said: "The foxes have holes, and the birds of the air have nests; but the Son of man hath not where to lay his head" (Matt. 8:20). To those who would be tempted to give him second place, he reminded: "If any man come to me, and hate not his father, and mother, and wife, and children, and brethren, and sisters, yea, and his own life also, he cannot be my disciple" (Luke 14:26). To those who would yield to indulgence he warned: "And if thy right eye offend thee, pluck it out, and cast it from thee: for it is profitable for thee that one of thy members should perish, and not that thy whole body should be cast into hell" (Matt.

5 : 29). To his men who were clamoring for places of privilege in his kingdom he offered "a cup of suffering" and "a baptism of death." "But Jesus answered and said, Ye know not what ye ask. Are ye able to drink of the cup that I shall drink of, and to be baptized with the baptism that I am baptized with?" (Matt. 20:22).

How strange this sounds to us in our eagerness to measure our success in terms of numbers and bigness and popular approval. Not once did Jesus lower his demands to appease the crowd or to get a single follower. The inquisitive came gaping, just as they would have come to an accident or a dog fight. The self-seekers resolved to take the tide of his popularity at the flood, and ride on to fortune. Patriots, restive under the dominion of Rome, were eager to use him as a firebrand of revolution. Many were stirred to impulsive enthusiasm. A few were conscious of the brooding of the Spirit. In one way or another he said to them, "If any man will come after me, let him deny himself, and take up his cross, and follow me" (Matt. 16:24).

2. Christ and His Cross

This high call to Christian discipleship springs from the deep truth that at the heart of God's purpose for Christ was his cross. It was a law as deep as life.

Christ's lifelong temptation was not the downward pull to moral degradation. It was his struggle between the cross or some easier way to win the world. He was aware of his power, unlimited. "If you be the Son of God," was Satan's subtle word, and he was, "then use that power to capture men's loyalty by satisfying their hunger with bread or dazzle them with the spectacular and the external or let the forces of this world place the crown of dominion on your head." This is one way to win a following, to build a kingdom. The alternative is the way of the cross. Which way? This was his temptation. This was his struggle.

Well does Dr. Kerr say it: "That is the temptation. That is the only temptation, and the artist has rightly interpreted the conflict that possessed the soul of Jesus. Will it be a life that counts for self and for world prestige, or will it be a life that loses itself in service to others? Will it be a crown that stands for force or shall it be a cross that stands for love? There is no other temptation." [6]

As Jesus' life began and continued in agony around the cross so did it come to its glorious climax. He faced the issue once again in the shadows of Gethsemane and settled it once and for all. "O my Father, if it be possible, let this cup pass from me: nevertheless not as I will, but as thou wilt" (Matt. 26:39). On the following day that prayer was answered on a hill called Calvary. The cross became God's and his and ours!

3. *The Christian and His Cross*

The cross has become the symbol of the voluntary, self-giving, sacrificial life and love of our Lord Jesus Christ. It has become, also, the symbol of our discipleship.

Unless we accept what Christ has done for us on his cross, life in him cannot begin for us. That we have tried to make clear and profoundly believe. All must say with Paul: "I have been crucified with Christ; it is no longer I who live, but Christ who lives in me; and the life I now live in the flesh I live by faith in the Son of God, who loved me and gave himself for me" (Gal. 2:20, RSV). The higher self can never live unless the lower self, the sinful self is nailed to his cross.

"Nevertheless, I live . . ." and the life we live must be motivated, characterized by the principle of the cross. Our cross is not, as we sometimes mistakenly believe, a burden, a tragedy thrust upon us. It is the voluntary acceptance of Christ's way of life as our own. Christ calls upon us to make it a daily experience.

What does it mean in terms of daily life? It means "denying ourselves." It means saying no to our own desires, our own way when they stand in conflict with his way. As one has put it: "Denying ourselves means far more than refusing to give things to ourselves. Self-denial, in a common use of the term, is abstaining from certain luxuries . . . The denial of self is something deeper. It is making ourselves not an end, but a means, in the kingdom of God. It is subordinating the clamoring ego, with its shrill claim for priority, its preoccupation with 'I,' 'me,' and 'mine,' its concern for self-assertion, its insistence on comfort and prestige; denying self, not for the sake of denial as a sort of moral athletics, but for Christ's sake, for the sake of putting the self into his cause." [7]

It means giving up our prejudice, our spirit of bigotry, our selfish claims to make way for an inclusive, compassionate Christian love.

It means assuming our share of the world's burden—losing ourselves that others may find life, dying that others may live. This cross we must take up as Christ took his—for the sake of others. "We are conscripted to carry a burden: burdens are the 'thousand natural shocks that flesh is heir to.' But we volunteer to carry a cross, as seems to be implied in take up, for a cross is somebody else's burden or the suffering which we choose to endure for Christ's truth." [8]

Nothing, I think, does the world need more than a demonstration of the cross as a redemptive way of life. We must be willing to suffer for his sake and others. For if human suffering is ever to be redeemed it will be because human beings, inspired and sustained by a vision of the will and the work of God, are willing to be used toward that end.

After Adoniram Judson was released from prison in Burma he bore deep scars on his wrists made by the iron shackle. When a request was made for men to go to a neighboring province to preach the gospel the king's reply was: "Send your preachers, my people will not hear them. But do not send the man with the scars. They cannot withstand the scars!" A selfish world will ever find it difficult to withstand the scars of sacrificial love.

The real struggle for the Christian is not always—or perhaps the most crucial—with the downward call of low living. It is with the acceptance of Jesus' cross as our way of life. "If any man will come after me, let him . . . take up his cross, . . ." It is the continuing struggle on the high road of Christian living.

FOR FURTHER STUDY AND DISCUSSION

1. For a fuller discussion of the idea of "salvation as a continuing experience," see Dr. W. T. Conner's book, *The Gospel of Redemption*, chapter 4.
2. Use Bunyan's *Pilgrim's Progress* to discover the age-old enemies with which a Christian must contend in his journey to the Celestial City.
3. Discuss the nature of Christ's temptations. What was the real issue in his lifelong struggle?
4. Discuss some of the issues facing us today in which we as Christians have an opportunity to share in the experience of cross-bearing.

CHAPTER 4 OUTLINE

I. THE GOAL OF MATURITY—THE FULNESS OF CHRIST

   1. That Man May Know God

   2. That Man May Know Himself

   3. That Man May Become Christlike

II. THE PATTERN OF MATURITY—GROW UP IN EVERY WAY

   1. Physical Maturity

   2. Mental Maturity

   3. Spiritual Maturity

III. THE POWER FOR MATURITY—SOURCES OF STRENGTH

   1. Worship—the Recovery of Awareness

   2. The Bible—the Living Word

   3. Prayer—the Secret Life

4

Growing Toward Spiritual Maturity— the New Resources

LIFE is like a mountain and a river. The mountains stand there against the sky—symbols of that which is unchanging, eternal. From those mountains flows a river. It, too, is always there, yet never the same. It flows on from day to day—finding new depths, rushing over unpredictable obstacles, into eddies and quiet pools, around sharp turns and through wide valleys. Always it is flowing toward the same distant fulness. Wherever it goes it refreshes and renews.

That is the Christian life at its best. It flows from the eternal. It must be fed constantly by those everlasting springs. It is never a stagnant pool. Its nature is movement toward a more distant goal.

In the previous chapters we have written of the eternal purpose, the new beginning, the onward struggle. In them there is the changeless God and the ever-changing life. Now we come to focus our attention on the goal. What is it in the onward-flowing Christian life that we hope to achieve?

I. THE GOAL OF MATURITY—THE FULNESS OF CHRIST

What did God have in mind for man? What kind of a person did he intend him to be? How did he plan for him to live his life? By what standard could a man measure himself? There is no finer answer to these questions than Paul's word in his Ephesian letter. He is writing about God's purpose for the church but, within the framework of the church, for the individual. He says, "until we all attain to the unity of the faith and of the knowledge of the Son of God, to mature

47

manhood, to the measure of the stature of the fulness of Christ" (Eph. 4:13, RSV). That is the measure and the goal of life within time. "The measure of the stature of the fulness of Christ." Or, to put it in our terms, to achieve mature Christian character is to find the fulfilment of life's highest destiny.

1. *That Man May Know God*

Slowly God made himself known to man. Through the power of his creative work, by his guiding and sustaining providence, by his acts of deliverance he revealed himself. In the mind of man God's great attributes took shape—his unlimited power and wisdom, his brooding presence, his holiness, his righteousness, his love. Although these belonged to God who was both eternally supreme and intensely personal, he was yet far removed beyond man's capacity to see or understand.

Then in the fulness of time God moved into human history. In Christ God became man. His divine attributes were clothed in a human personality. Christ did not come simply to teach truths about God. He brought God near in a human life. He was God stepping out of the frame of eternity into the front room of life. He revealed God as a person. He showed men what God was really like in his character. His life was God's power and holiness and love in action. His attitude toward men was God's attitude. Indeed, as Jesus said, "He that hath seen me hath seen the Father" (John 14:9).

As Dr. Phillips says, "We cannot hold too big a conception of God, but the more our hearts and minds and imaginations are used, the more astounding becomes the central fact of our faith—that so infinite a God allowed himself to be, so to speak, scaled down to fit the narrow limits of humanity. For all his vastness and mystery, he has made himself known in an unforgettable character by which all men can see what sort of Person it is 'with whom we have to do' (Heb. 4:13)." [1]

If then our goal is to be like Christ in our character, it is to be like God who sent him.

2. *That Man May Know Himself*

Christ not only brought God down close enough for man to see; he lifted man high enough for him to see himself.

Into the life of man came *The Man*—Jesus of Nazareth. Men watched him grow, were impressed by his humble and unselfish spirit, saw him perform his deeds of love and mercy, watched him under fire, beheld him suffer and die. At last they saw him conquer death to give validity and eternal meaning to such a life. He sent them on their way singing: "This is to live; this is the life; this is what God meant for man to be—and do. This is the life that can never die." Paul summed it up in his own words—and life, "For to me to live is Christ" (Phil. 1:21). There can be no greater goal, no higher purpose than that. Christ was God's man, he was man's man. He was the God-man, the true man, the Son of man. He was representative of all men. He was the measure of every man. Sidney Lanier describes him thus:

> But Thee, but Thee, O sovereign Seer of Time,
> But Thee, O poet's Poet, Wisdom's Tongue,
> But Thee, O man's best Man, O love's best Love,
> O perfect life in perfect labor writ,
> O all men's Comrade, Servant, King, or Priest—
> What if and yet, what mole, what flaw, what lapse,
> What least defect or shadow of defect,
> What rumor, tattled by an enemy,
> Of inference loose, what lack of grace
> Even in torture's grasp, or sleep's, or death's—
> Oh, what amiss may I forgive in Thee,
> Jesus, good Paragon, thou Crystal Christ?

3. *That Man May Become Christlike*

To achieve a Christlike character has been the goal of every true Christian. It became the obsession of the great

Apostle's life. Hear him as he bares his soul against the ever-challenging yet ever-receding height. "For his sake I have suffered the loss of all things, and count them as refuse, in order that I may gain Christ" (Phil. 3:8, RSV). Like Paul we too desire to lay hold upon him for ourselves—to be like him in all ways. Like Paul also we know that we shall never attain —in this life. But there is no other goal worthy of our utmost.

Only as man reaches for the unattainable does his life grow. Striving for the highest his own soul finds new dimensions. There is no stopping place. Christ is the "pioneer of life." He is ever going before us, blazing new trails, inviting us to come up higher. "See what love the Father has given us, that we should be called children of God; and so we are . . . Beloved, we are God's children now; it does not yet appear what we shall be, but we know that when he appears we shall be like him, for we shall see him as he is" (1 John 3:1–2, RSV). That is the goal of character. That is what man at last by God's grace can become.

II. THE PATTERN OF MATURITY—GROW UP IN EVERY WAY

The Christian goal of life is mature manhood—the stature of the fulness of Christ—that is the maturity manifest in the manhood of Christ. The pattern of that development is that we shall "*grow up in every way*." There is to be no area of our life underdeveloped or undeveloped. This is God's way for us to escape the tragedy of being spiritual dwarfs all our lives. How meaningful is Dr. W. O. Carver's paraphrase of Paul's word to the Ephesians: ". . . that we shall no longer be content to remain babes, lacking responsibility, understanding, and intelligent self-direction toward our goal, mere tossing waves and carried around here and there without aim or order by every chance wind of teaching," that "we shall ever be growing, in all ways and all respects into full relation and co-ordination with him who is the Head . . ." (Eph. 4:15–16, Carver).

This was the pattern Jesus set for us in his own life. Luke tells us that when Jesus, at twelve, returned with his parents from Jerusalem to Nazareth, he "increased in wisdom and stature, and in favour with God and man" (Luke 2:52).

Nothing is said about Jesus' physical size or appearance— perhaps because it did not especially impress people. His growing wisdom was not primarily in the accumulation of facts. His social status had nothing to do with making the "social register" of his day. His growth certainly was quantitative, but far more important, it was qualitative. He developed and used all the powers of his great life. Although he lived only thirty-three years, he lived *all* his life; he lived it to the fullest.

If we are to "grow up in every way," we, too, must discover new dimensions for life. Many of us use only a small part of our actual capacities. We need to add fulness to our years, insight to our knowledge, spirituality to our creeds, and compassion to our social existence. Our growth should be in the measure of the fulness of him into whose likeness we grow.

1. *Physical Maturity*

There never seems to be a time when we are not conscious of our physical growth. Little boys and girls can hardly wait until they grow up. They do everything they can to hurry it along, including the wearing of grown-up things, and, unfortunately, taking on grown-up habits! Older people become conscious of their growth in the other direction. They buy pills by the millions to slow it down!

As Christians we should be concerned about the physical. It is the vehicle that God has given us through which we are to express ourselves. It is a part of the wholeness of life. Strong, healthy bodies are essential to living in this physical universe.

Jesus not only enjoyed normal, physical growth himself, but he was deeply concerned about the physical well-being of others. He fed the hungry and was called "The Bread of Life." He healed the sick and was known as "The Great Physician." Wherever his message has gone institutions of healing and physical care have followed—hospitals, orphanages, homes for the aged. He cared deeply about man's physical needs.

Even more significant, Jesus has taught us how to put the physical in its proper place in the wholeness of life. He did not divide life into the sacred and the secular. All of life was sacred. The fields and flowers, the seed and soil, the birds and beasts became teachers of God's care. Paul thought of the body as something sacred. "Do you not know that your body is a temple of the Holy Spirit within you, which you have from God? You are not your own" (1 Cor. 6:19, RSV). God saw fit to use the body—in truth all physical things—to reveal his glory. But he was master of the physical, never its servant. So he would have us to keep it in its proper place. "Seek ye first the kingdom of God, and his righteousness; and all these things shall be added unto you" (Matt. 6:33).

2. *Mental Maturity*

Being retarded mentally is even a greater tragedy than being physically handicapped. Often it is not of our choosing. Those who have this limitation must ever have our deepest compassion. Here again, we believe that Jesus reached in with his power to give peace to "demon possessed," twisted minds. Perhaps at long last doors are beginning to open for us in the ministry of healing sick minds as well as sick bodies.

Our concern at this point, however, is for those who do not or will not use the minds they have. Most of us use only a small percentage of our actual mental acumen. Again and again Jesus came up against the "dullness" of his disciples. They were mentally unresponsive to his teaching. No wonder he gave fully a third of his active ministry to the training of the twelve. It was not enough that they should have the facts.

They had those. It was insight into their meaning that they so sadly lacked. They must grow in their ability to understand and interpret the facts. One of the greatest needs of our day— or any day—is the insight to interpret the meaning of life and the events sweeping about us—especially in the light of God's purpose.

The mind, even more than the body, is difficult to bring under control. It is the source of much that destroys the wholeness of life. Jesus looked to the mind rather than the body as the real culprit in our evil deeds. "What comes out of the mouth proceeds from the heart, and this defiles a man" (Matt. 15:18, RSV).

The mind is the battleground for the civil war within us. It is the citadel that is besieged by our fears and anxieties and tension and the far greater enemies that make us psychiatric patients. The mind is imprisoned by our ignorance and prejudices.

Paul refused to let his mind be dominated by its circumstances or imprisoned by iron bars. Writing from his cell in Rome to the Philippian Christians he says, "Finally, brethren, whatever is true, whatever is honorable, whatever is just, whatever is pure, whatever is lovely, whatever is gracious, if there is any excellence, if there is anything worthy of praise, think about these things" (Phil. 4:8, RSV).

Jesus urged us to bring our total lives under the reign of his love. "Thou shalt love the Lord thy God with all thy heart and with all thy soul, and with all thy mind" (Matt. 22:37). We must let him be the master of our minds. We must let him use our minds to their fullest capacity. We cannot grow up into the mature manhood of Christ until we become mature in our thinking.

3. *Spiritual Maturity*

Life cannot be separated into compartments. To grow up in every way means to grow up together. A man may be a physical giant and a mental moron. He may be a mental wizard and a spiritual pigmy. Indeed, the greatest tragedy of today is that we are growing taller, living longer, knowing more, but we are spiritually illiterate. We are technologically mature—but spiritually adolescent.

To grow up physically with a stunted mind is tragic. To grow up physically and mentally with a spirit left untamed and untended is both sad and dangerous. It is displeasing to God.

What does it mean to grow up spiritually? Luke says of Jesus that he increased in favor with God. Certainly, he was never out of favor with God. As he grew into mature manhood he increased in his understanding of the Father's purpose for his life, his own redemptive mission, and the meaning of God's will. So even at the time of his baptism God could say, "This is my beloved Son, with whom I am well pleased" (Matt. 3:17, RSV).

We, too, must mature in the spiritual qualities of life. Our sense of spiritual insight into God's purpose and will should become increasingly clear. Our faith in God should become stronger. We should learn how to be more patient. We should know better how to handle life's restraints. We should grow up in our attitude toward others. We should become increasingly fruitful in all the qualities of the Spirit: "love, joy, peace, patience, kindness, goodness, faithfulness, gentleness, self-control" (Gal. 5:22-23, RSV). The greatest of all is love—Christian love. No quality is more comprehensive than this. We should be constantly growing in love until we come to the point as Paul said: "that Christ may dwell in your hearts through faith; that you, being rooted and grounded in love, may have power to comprehend with all the saints what is the breadth and length and height and depth, and to know the love of Christ which surpasses knowledge, that you may be filled with all the fulness of God" (Eph. 3:17-19, RSV).

III. THE POWER FOR MATURITY—SOURCES OF STRENGTH

The river of life, flowing onward to its ultimate destiny must ever find its source in the height of the Eternal. Or, to change the figure, the tree bears its fruit because of the silent, vital life within—drawn from the roots, the soil, the sun.

The Christian life springs from God—from him, too, it goes on growing in grace. We must not conclude, however, that growth toward Christian maturity is without effort on our part. The plant of life must be nourished, cultivated, watered.

Someone has described an atheist as a man with no invisible means of support. It could well be the description of the average, secularized American. We are trying to live entirely on our visible means of support. We are enjoying fruits of a Christian civilization without realizing their source and without claiming the source for ourselves.

When we accept Christ we no longer have to depend upon human nature alone for our resources. We become partakers of his nature. We draw upon this new life within us which is made available when we become the children of God.

God has made available for us sources of strength—capacities by which we can lay hold of spiritual reality that the "inner life" may be quickened and fed.

1. *Worship—the Recovery of Awareness*

Since man was created he had felt the need and found a way to bow in the spirit of reverence and pay homage and make sacrifice to the One in whose image he is made. Worship is both instinctive and universal because of who man is. Just as man must have food and water and air because he is a body, so he must worship because he is a living soul.

When we speak of worship we mean much more than attending "a worship service in our church." That is vitally important, and unless we cultivate the spirit of reverence and awareness there it is not likely that we shall have it else-where. Granted, there are times when those services are a great disappointment. The music is terrible, the sermon is worse. Everything seems to go wrong. There is much "sound and fury, signifying nothing." But in spite of such experiences there are times when God with whom we have to do is there, closer than hands and feet, the very breath of life itself. We have united our hearts in prayer, in listening to his Word, in singing the hymns of praise. We have confessed our sins, received forgiveness and strength, and expressed our highest joys. We go away feeling that it was good to have been there—God was in that place, and we met him and knew him.

That is what makes worship vital—in a church service or anywhere. It is to recover the awareness of his presence. Moses found him at the burning bush and heard him say, "Put off thy shoes from off thy feet, for the place whereon thou standest is holy ground" (Ex. 3:5). Jacob was aware of his presence that night on the stony ground of Luz: "And Jacob awaked out of his sleep, and he said, Surely the Lord is in this place; and I knew it not" (Gen. 28:16). Isaiah saw him in a time of crises as he worshiped in the great Temple: "In the year that king Uzziah died I saw also the Lord sitting upon a throne, high and lifted up, and his train filled the temple" (Isa. 6:1).

It is this awareness that Jesus said must be at the very heart of worship—not a special place or time or people. To the Samaritan woman he said. "Woman, believe me, the hour cometh, when ye shall neither in this mountain, nor yet at Jerusalem, worship the Father . . . But the hour cometh, and now is, when the true worshippers shall worship the Father in spirit and in truth: for the Father seeketh such to worship him. God is a Spirit: and they that worship him must worship him in spirit and in truth" (John 4:21-24).

Do you know the story of Sidney Lanier? A spirit of rever-ence for life and constant awareness led him in his frail physical health to find renewed strength. He fought his unequal battle with disease, fighting the enemy day by day and year by year; but no repining there, no sorrow there, no complaint there—only optimism, cheer, hopefulness and triumph.

The secret of it all was that in the wilderness through which he passed there was God. He did not have to wait till life's fitful fever was over, but there in Georgia, in Baltimore at the Peabody, at Brunswick where emaciated, dying, he watched the marsh hens build their nests in the marsh grass, we hear him singing of the greatness of God.

> As the marsh-hen secretly builds on the watery sod,
> Behold I will build me a nest on the greatness of God:
> I will fly in the greatness of God as the marsh-hen flies
> In the freedom that fills all the space 'twixt the marsh
>   and the skies:
> By so many roots as the marsh-grass sends in the sod,
> I will heartily lay me a-hold on the greatness of God:
> Oh, like to the greatness of God is the greatness within
> The range of the marshes, the liberal marshes of Glynn.

Here, too, we can find strength for our lives—in worship service or out of it—for God is wherever men will open their eyes and see him. And having seen him, their souls reach like growing plants toward the light. They become better men in his presence. They become aware of the needs of others. They come to great moments of dedication in which each responds to God's call: "Here am I; send me."

2. *The Bible—the Living Word*

What an inexhaustible treasure the Bible is! As literature its value is unsurpassed. Its incomparable stories will live on and on as we share them with our children and their children until the end of time. Above all, it is the story of God's dealings with men, the record of the revelation of his eternal, redemptive purpose for mankind. It reaches its climax in the life and death and resurrection of his son, Jesus Christ. It points the way of his continuing purpose in time through the work of his Holy Spirit until the consummation of his purpose beyond history. To be intelligent people, we should know the Bible. Our minds should be enlightened by its truths.

For our purposes here, however, we should think of it as the medium of God's written word to open to us his living Word. We are not worshipers of the Bible. We worship him of whom the Bible speaks. We need to know the facts of the Bible but we also need to know the Author of the Bible. Jesus said to the carping critics of his day: "You search the scriptures, because you think that in them you have eternal life; and it is they that bear witness to me; yet you refuse to come to me that you may have life" (John 5:39–40, RSV). It was the warmth and strength of his presence that his Emmaus disciples found as he walked with them along the way. "They said to each other, 'Did not our hearts burn within us while he talked to us on the road, while he opened to us the scriptures?'" (Luke 24:32, RSV).

As we open the Book let us open our minds to understand, our hearts to feel, and yield our wills to obey the Life that speaks from its pages.

> Break Thou the bread of life, Dear Lord, to me,
> As Thou didst break the loaves beside the sea;
> Beyond the sacred page I seek Thee, Lord;
> My spirit pants for Thee, O living Word.

3. Prayer—the Secret Life

Prayer is like a beautiful rose—to begin to define it, to analyze it you destroy its beauty. Margaret Slattery gives us this unforgettable story that says more than all of our reasonable philosophies.

"A simple New England church on the hill and entering its open door a man who has parked his expensive streamlined car under the maples by the side of the road. It is Friday. He will spend the week end with friends.

"Through the clear windows the sun shines upon the red carpet on the aisle, and the glistening white pews. It rests upon the great Bible, open on the pulpit. No cross, no incense, no sacred symbols—only silence and a Presence.

"The man seats himself in the last pew in the farthest corner. He is alone in the little white church. He bows his head upon his hands. Minutes pass—

"Now he is leaving the little church. He walks slowly toward the maples and his car. But he seems not at all like the man who entered the church less than a half hour ago. His shoulders are squared. Something has happened to the sad, strained eyes that this year have looked first upon heavy financial loss and then upon death.

"What could have happened to him there in the silence of the church. A miracle! Only those who pray can describe it. But they *know*." [2]

Jesus talked but little about prayer; he prayed much. From his prayer life there came a quiet serenity, a superb power that caused those who knew him to try to discover the secret. Dr. George Buttrick writes: "Indeed examination almost drives us to the conclusion that prayer was the vital secret. Let us be blunt: some of his words had been already spoken by others, and much of the letter of his teaching was not new. The stress, here central, here marginal, was new; but not the letter. Yet words that were dead on other lips became electric on his lips. Why? Indeed others had done what he had done, and there had been perhaps a hundred crosses raised on Golgotha. But other men's death on a cross left it still a dead tree, while his cross became alive unto eternal life. Yes, there were factors at work that go forth from the throne of God. Yet not without the lonely prayers of Jesus. The disciples believed that prayer was his secret: 'Lord, teach us to pray.'" [3]

Prayer, too, became the secret of their own lives. Faced with the task of carrying out his mission and winning a pagan world, they waited and prayed to be filled with the power of his Spirit. They prayed until self and danger were alike forgotten, until God came—like tongues of fire, we are told: like mighty rushing wind, like rivers of living water, like sudden speech to a man born dumb. Perhaps it would be foolish to literalize the experience, but it would be still more foolish to deny or diminish it. Perhaps each could have said, as Browning once said:

> Where one heard noise,
> And one saw flame
> I only knew He named my name.

Those men of the early church had no timid, little half-faith in prayer. They knew that prayer was opening life to all the cleansing power of God. Their prayer redeemed their eyes so that they suddenly understood Jesus and his cosmic cross; it widened their sympathies so that they called the stranger their brother; it canceled their greed so that they "had all things in common," and it turned their fear into such courage of eternal life that they cared little whether they lived or died. Are you going to say, cringingly, of prayer: "We can at least pray"? On the Great Divide is a little lake. It is landlocked in dry weather. But in rains it flows down both sides of the mountains and waters every plain. Prayer gives the overflow. Those men prayed.

Prayer must become the secret of our lives if we are to grow into a life of power and usefulness that is akin to the manhood of the Master. Through prayer we affirm our faith in God. We open our lives to him at regular times and in special ways but keep our lives open to him at all times. We pray without ceasing. We let him be in our lives and thoughts as we work and play and worship. Above all, we place ourselves in his hands to do his will, for the greatest of all prayers is this: "Not my will but thine be done." To pray like that is to find strength for whatever is ahead. It involves a great risk,

for his will may be for you and me, as it was for him, a cross.
But if it is, his strength will transform it into a life of victory.

> Lord, what a change within us one short hour
> Spent in Thy presence will prevail to make!
> What heavy burdens from our bosoms take,
> What parched grounds refresh as with a shower!
> We kneel, and all around us seems to lower;
> We rise, and all, the distant and the near,
> Stands forth in sunny outline brave and clear;
> We kneel, how weak! We rise, how full of power!
> Why, therefore, should we do ourselves this wrong,
> Or others, that we are not always strong,
> That we are ever overborne with care,
> That we should ever weak or heartless be,
> Anxious or troubled, when with us is prayer,
> And joy and strength and courage are with Thee!

FOR FURTHER STUDY AND DISCUSSION

1. Several excellent books are available for additional study. We would suggest especially: *Into the Same Image*, R. E. O. White; *Ephesians: Patterns for Christian Living*, Ray Sumners; *Tap Roots for Tall Souls*, Loftin Hudson; *The Character of Jesus*, Charles Jefferson.
2. Have someone tell the story of Charles M. Sheldon's classic story, *In His Steps*.
3. Discuss the amount of time and effort we are giving to the mental and physical development of our children as compared to the time given to their spiritual development.
4. Secure from our Sunday School Board and elsewhere suggested materials for use in private and family devotions and discuss ways that they along with the Bible may be used effectively.

CHAPTER 5 OUTLINE

I. WHAT IS THE CHURCH?

  1. The Continuing Incarnation
  2. The New Testament Conception
  3. Word Pictures of the Church

II. WHO BELONGS TO THE CHURCH?

  1. The Church Belongs to Christ
  2. Members Who Do Not Belong
  3. The Fellowship of the Living

III. WHAT THE CHURCH CAN MEAN TO EACH MEMBER

  1. The Church Can Help Each Member Know
  2. The Church Can Help Each Member Grow
  3. The Church Can Help Each Member Keep
     in Touch with the Source of Life

IV. WHAT WE CAN MEAN TO THE CHURCH

  1. We Should Be Grateful for Its Heritage
  2. We Can Stand for Its Faith
  3. We Can Share in Its Responsibility

5

Becoming a Responsible Church Member—the New Fellowship

MAN was not made to live alone. To live and reproduce his kind he must be a part of a family. He is made for fellowship. There is a part of him that never develops except as it is shared with others. He never reaches his highest possibilities outside of the social unit. Progress for every man is dependent upon the members of the community living and working together. The birds of the air, the bees that swarm, the ants in their highly organized dwellings teach us the sense of community—indeed, the necessity for community.

The church is designed for the spirit of togetherness. It is for the fellowship of those who share a common experience in Jesus Christ. It is God's design. The church is not an "afterthought" that came along because somebody decided we needed such an organization.

It is a part of God's plan for the ages. Dr. W. O. Carver says: "The universal church and its local manifestations as congregations are distinctly divine in origin and in meaning. They are God's creation, the people of God, and of his Christ. They constitute a new humanity produced, preserved, and empowered as God's representative in the midst of 'all the families of the earth.' The church is the congregation of the true Israel of God, continuing, interpreting, and supplanting the Old Testament Israel in terms of God's saints in Christ Jesus.' " [1]

We trace the church back, then, to God's nature and to his purpose for us and for our world. He needed it to achieve his purpose. We need it for our highest spiritual development.

I. What Is the Church?

What comes into your mind when we say, "the church"? It means different things to different people. Some think of the building in which the church meets—the little white frame building in the country or the great Gothic stone structure "where cross the crowded ways of life." To others the church is erroneously thought of as a particular sect or denomination, such as Methodist, Baptist, Presbyterian. Or, it is an institution like the school or the government. Or, again, in the minds of some it may be just another organization like a club, a lodge, or a social agency.

What is the church? Perhaps its very familiarity makes it difficult to describe. As someone has suggested, "A giraffe is easier to draw than a dog, and a rhinoceros than a horse." But if we are to see the church as it really is, as it is in God's purpose and for man's good, we must try to know what it is.

1. *The Continuing Incarnation*

The church has its historic roots in the Old Testament. God's plan began with a man—called out, set apart for God's purpose. Then it included a family. Finally, it encompassed a nation. To that nation—Israel—he committed his purpose. Through her the nations of the earth would be blessed.

Israel's failure to completely fulfil that purpose is now history. But God's purpose would not fail. That purpose reached its climax in the incarnation: "God was in Christ, reconciling the world unto himself" (2 Cor. 5:19).

Through whom would God continue his work following the ascension of our Lord? We believe his redemptive purpose was to be carried on through his church—empowered, unified by his Holy Spirit. The writers of the New Testament consistently link the church—the new Israel—with Israel of the Old Testament.

The description of Israel in the plan of God in Exodus 19:4–6 is appropriated almost word for word in 1 Peter 2:9–10, as the description of those who believe in Christ: "But you are a chosen race, a royal priesthood, a holy nation, God's own people, that you may declare the wonderful deeds of him who called you out of darkness into his marvelous light. Once you were no people but now you are God's people; once you had not received mercy but now you have received mercy" (RSV).

Again W. O. Carver states with clarity this idea of God's unfolding purpose in what he calls the "*continuing incarnation*" through the church. "This new Israel was the new creation of God in Christ Jesus. It was to be the church of God in Christ Jesus . . . The congregation, a local manifestation of the church, begins in, and follows from, the fact that the total body of the redeemed constitutes the continuing, growing body of Christ. While the exact expression is never used, this comprehensive spiritual church is the continuation of the incarnation . . . The church, therefore, is God's 'new creation,' a new humanity in the midst of unredeemed humanity; a local church is a concrete embodiment of this church. The church is the extension of the incarnation. A local church is the manifestation of Christ in its community. The church is the body of Christ, who is himself the fulness of God in redemption; a local church is the functioning of the redeemed body in a fellowship of redeemed men." [2]

2. *The New Testament Conception*

Continuing this idea of the people of God "called out for a special purpose," the New Testament uses an interesting word which is translated "church." The Greek word is *ecclesia*. It is not a new word. It had been applied to citizens "called out" or "called into assembly" for various purposes (Acts 19:39). The writers of the New Testament used it to apply to the "called-out people of God," that is, the church. It is used 114 times altogether and in all but five instances it refers to the church.

In some instances the word is used in an inclusive or general sense. Such, for example, was the use when our Lord first applied it to his church. He said to Peter: "Upon this rock I will build my church" (Matt. 16:18). Various terms have been used to describe this general usage of the *ecclesia*. It has been called the "universal church" or the "transcendental community." Some have preferred to apply it to the church as an "institution." For example, we refer to "the home" when we do not have any home specifically in mind. The term "institution," however, like "organization," carries certain connotations that do not fit the church. In the truest sense it is neither an institution nor an organization. It is different; it possesses an inner life and spirit that make it unique. The church in this inclusive sense, applies to the whole body of believers. It takes in all those who have believed in Jesus Christ as Saviour and Lord.

In the majority of times the term is used it refers to "the local church," the church in Antioch or the church at Corinth, etc. This is the manifestation of the body of Christ in a specific place at a specific time. It is made up of a group of people who are voluntarily associated together because they share a common faith in Christ and are dedicated to the purpose of spreading his kingdom on earth.

3. *Word Pictures of the Church*

Today we do much of our reading in pictures. The pictorial magazine, the television have become vital media of communication. Jesus was a master at using pictures as a method of teaching. He drew lessons from the soil, the birds, the flowers. Paul, as well as others, used pictures to carry the message. There are three that applied especially to the church.

First, the church is referred to as *a building*. This is the image our Lord uses when he mentions his church for the first time. "Upon this rock I will build my church." A building, if it is to stand, must have a solid foundation. Paul says that foundation is Christ. "For other foundation can no man lay than that is laid, which is Jesus Christ" (1 Cor. 3:11).

Upon that foundation the church will rise. Peter conceived of himself and all believers as one of the stones. He speaks of them as "living stones." "Come to him, to that living stone, rejected by men but in God's sight chosen and precious; and like living stones be yourselves built into a spiritual house, to be a holy priesthood, to offer spiritual sacrifices acceptable to God through Jesus Christ" (1 Peter 2:4–5, RSV). This is the "stuff" then, out of which his church is to be built—men and women, like Peter who believe that "Jesus is the Christ, the Son of the living God." This is the faith that makes "dead material" into "living stones." As such it becomes the habitation of the Spirit of God.

The second picture which is used for the church is *the bride*. The language used to express the relation between Christ and his bride is as meaningful as it is beautiful. Paul expresses the hope that the church may so conduct herself in her earthly existence that she may in the end be presented as "a pure bride to her one husband." What fidelity that would be if the church could remain true to Christ and as Paul says, ". . . be presented before him in splendor, without spot or wrinkle or any such thing, that she might be holy and without blemish" (Eph. 5:27, RSV). In this sublime picture of the church as the bride, as the beloved of Christ, we see love at its best, loyalty at its highest.

The third picture used and, in many ways the greatest, is *the body* (1 Cor. 12:12–27). The church is the body of Christ. As such it is a living *organism*. It is not simply an institution. It is organized, but it is much more than an organization. As Emil Brunner says, the church uses an organization, but it is an organism. It is a fellowship of people bound together by a common life.

Christ is the head of the church (Col. 1:18). As such he is the directing mind and the living power that gives life and unity and purpose to the body. The body achieves its highest efficiency and true glory when it responds to his mind and spirit.

As we shall see later we become a part of his body when we become new creatures in Christ. While each member has a different and unique function, each is important. Each also needs the other. "If the whole body were an eye, where were the hearing? If the whole were hearing, where were the smelling? But now hath God set the members every one of them in the body, as it hath pleased him" (1 Cor. 12:17–18). They reach their highest good when they learn to work together. When one suffers they all suffer. They should all strive to work together to achieve harmony with him who is the head.

In these three pictures—and there are others—we get something of the strength and mystery and purpose of Christ's church. As the body of Christ as the "continuing incarnation," we shall be called upon to suffer for him, to live for him, to reveal him to the world.

II. WHO BELONGS TO THE CHURCH?

Do you belong to the church? That may seem like a strange question to ask, but the answer may not be as obvious as we think. It is high time that we all think more seriously about the matter of belonging to the church.

If we mean that we have gone through the "mechanics" of walking down the aisle on the invitation, answering the required questions on the application card, being voted on by the members of the congregation, yes, even being baptized, then we could answer in the affirmative—"I belong to the church." Sixty per cent of the people who live in the United States belong to some church, and that percentage is increasing every year. Thousands of people have their names inscribed on some church membership record. They belong—or do they? Let us try seriously to find an answer to that question. It is important; it is eternally important. For one of the gravest problems facing our churches today is not the unconverted people on the outside but the unconverted people on the inside!

1. *The Church Belongs to Christ*

The church does not come into existence simply by a group of people coming together to worship and study and serve. They may even have certain noble beliefs in common. This does not constitute a church. It can in no sense be brought into being by man's doing.

Jesus said to Simon Peter, "I will build my church." It belongs to him; the whole experience that led Peter to make his confession of faith was initiated by God. "And Jesus answered and said unto him, Blessed art thou, Simon Bar-jona: for flesh and blood hath not revealed it unto thee, but my Father which is in heaven" (Matt. 16:17). Peter's response to God's revelation, his acceptance of Jesus Christ as God's Son qualified him—and will qualify all, if it be a sincere commitment—to belong to his church.

That is to say we must first belong to Christ before we can belong to his church. As one puts it: "Apart from him there is no Church. We can neither create nor destroy a Church. It is not our Church. We cannot do with it what we like. We cannot say in it what we choose. We cannot use it for our own ends. It is Christ's Church. He is its builder and maker. It is his message that the Church proclaims. It is his salvation that the Church offers. It is in his presence that the Church rejoices. It is Christ's people who alone constitute the Church." [3]

2. *Members Who Do Not Belong*

That is our dilemma. We receive people into our member-ship, but they do not belong because they do not belong to Christ. They have never had the experience of the "new birth." They are not "new creatures" in Christ.

This problem raises a serious question. Can one be "a mem-ber" of a church and not be a Christian? Of course he can— thousands of unsaved people are in all our churches. Can one be a Christian and not be a member of the church? That de-pends on what we mean by "church," does it not? If we go on giving the old answer, of course, we must say, yes. Belong-ing to the church does not save a man. If, however, we con-ceive of the church as Paul did as "the body of Christ," then if one *is a Christian,* he *is a member of Christ's body.* He so became when he had the experience that brought him into a saving union with Jesus Christ.

This is the meaning Billy Graham has in mind when he says: "Now that you have accepted Christ as your Savior and put your trust and confidence in Him, you have already be-come a member of the great universal church. You are a member of the household of faith. You are a part of the body of Christ. Now you are called upon to obey Christ, and if you obey Christ, you will follow His example of joining with others in the worship of God. It has been said, 'In practical terms this membership of the body of Christ must actually mean membership of some local manifestation of his body in the church.' " [4]

The choice to join the individual congregation—the local church in time and place—is ours to make when we accept Christ as Saviour and Lord. We belong to his body when we belong to him—and not until then.

3. *The Fellowship of the Living*

One of the wonders and glories of the church is that it is

made up of all kinds of people—people from every cultural, economic, educational, and social background. They are not perfect people. More often, they are weak and ordinary people.

A man once stood on the church steps watching a congregation assemble for worship. He knew most of them well. One by one they went up the steps and through the door—a pretty sorry bunch of folk, thought the man. Weak men and women, some of them spineless in character, others full of deceit. Get them all together and you've got a sad assembly! The whole is just as great as the sum of its parts. But then this man went into the church, joined the company in fellowship, felt the invisible "plus" element added to the sum of the whole. In Christ, this man discovered, the whole is greater than the sum of its parts. Fellowship exceeds the law of mathematics. As they stood to sing "My Faith Looks Up to Thee" the man was sure that something more than a company of frail men and women was in that room. In true fellowship is a lifting and delivering power that hell cannot bind.

In truth those people had "come alive" in Christ. The Holy Spirit had transformed them from a social group subject to the laws of other assemblies into a living, spiritual fellowship—*kionōnia*. That is what makes a church a church. It is made up of those to whom the risen Christ has imparted his Spirit. It is the fellowship of those who believe in the resurrection, and to whom the living Christ is real. The church is the new people of God, made possible by the death and resurrection of Jesus, and created by his Spirit living in their midst.

In his play, *A Servant in the House*, Charles Rann Kennedy describes the church as "a living thing." He says: "The Church has to be seen in a certain way, under certain conditions. Some people never see it at all. You must understand, this is no dead pile of stones and unmeaning timber. It is a living thing. When you enter it you hear a sound—a sound as of some mighty poem chanted. Listen long enough, and you will learn that it is made up of the beating of human hearts, of the nameless music of men's souls—that is, if you have ears. If you have eyes, you will presently see the church itself—a looming mystery of many shapes and shadows, leaping sheer from the floor to the dome. The work of no ordinary builder!" [5]

This is the rich and abiding fellowship that we enjoy when we, in the truest and deepest reality, belong to the church. It is his Spirit that makes possible the experience that we would share with the world.

III. What the Church Can Mean to Each Member

How wisely God has planned for his children. When a baby is born into the world it is born into a setting that is prepared to care for it until it can make its way alone. If that home is what God meant for it to be, it has been allowed months to prepare for the baby's arrival. At the time of birth wise parents begin immediately to do all that is necessary to see to it that this child develops normally and completely in all its capacities—physically, mentally, spiritually.

The church is God's counterpart to the home for his spiritual children. In its broadest term the church has a twofold responsibility. It is to reach and win those outside to an acceptance of Jesus Christ as Saviour and Lord. Once they have made that decision the church's responsibility does not end. We are to provide the opportunity and leadership necessary to establish them in the Christian way of life. The first we have done. We have laid great stress on evangelism—and rightly so. We have not been so successful in the second.

It does little good to compile statistics of those who have not stayed by their profession of faith or bemoan the fact that there are many inactive members on our church rolls. We need to assume our responsibility to try to do a better job in helping them "grow up in Christ in every way."

1. *The Church Can Help Each Member Know*

Because of our strong conviction that a personal experience with Jesus Christ is the only basis for belonging to the church we have shied away from classes of preparation for church membership. We can still be true to this conviction and also provide classes of orientation for those who have accepted Christ and, for that matter, for all who come into our church the first time.

The best time to begin this instruction is immediately following their decision. Someone from the staff or the membership can be made responsible for this service. Instruction classes can be arranged—one for those of Junior age and another for those above, preferably before baptism for those who are to be baptized. At least two class periods—more if desired—should be held for each group. Large groups are not essential. Sometimes the best teaching can be done with one or two persons. The classes can be kept functioning continuously for those coming into the church.

What shall we help them know in these orientation or initial instruction periods? There should be at least four general areas. First, we should help them understand better the conversion experience. If they have been in Sunday school or been brought up in a Christian home, they know the gospel story. They need to understand more fully what God in Christ has done for their salvation and what happened to them when they responded in repentance and faith to him. In other words, they need a clear understanding of what is involved in becoming a Christian—both for themselves and their future witness.

Second, they need an understanding of some of our basic Christian beliefs and some of our distinctive Baptist doctrines. There should be some justification for their joining a Baptist church.

Third, new members should become acquainted with the

local church which they have joined—its history, its buildings, its program, and its opportunities.

Fourth, they should know something of the church in its wider fellowship—how we work with other Baptist churches in the association, state, and Southern Baptist Convention. This would include our state, home, and foreign mission programs. They should be led also to see our relationship with other Christian groups with whom we have much in common.

It is true that we are attempting to cover a lot of territory in a short time; at least, it is a beginning. It is far better than nothing at all. There are excellent books which can be placed in their hands—or a church may prepare one of its own. It should be understood that this is but an introductory step that would lead into the total and continuous training program of the church.

2. *The Church Can Help Each Member Grow*

The church's program is not something that some "armchair strategist" thought up and superimposed upon it. We find its basic pattern in the New Testament. "Those who received his word were baptized, and there were added that day about three thousand souls. And they devoted themselves to the apostles' teaching and fellowship, to the breaking of bread and the prayers" (Acts 2:41-42, RSV). As the spiritual needs of the people arose the program developed to meet those needs. That principle has prevailed in the past and continues to prevail.

There is the need for us to know the Bible. This is the source Book for our faith and practice. In addition to individual study, the Sunday school seeks to meet that need in a teaching program for every age group under the best possible circumstances, with trained leaders and the latest methods and material for the teaching process.

There is a growing need for trained leaders and members who can give a reason for their faith. The church seeks to meet that need in the Training Union program on Sunday and in the specialized courses throughout the calendar year.

There is a need for us to know what's going on beyond our church in our mission work—a need to prepare our young people to hear God's call to special fields of Christian service. To meet this need the church provides the Brotherhood and Royal Ambassador programs for its men and boys and the Woman's Missionary Society and its auxiliaries for the women and girls.

There is a need for the strengthening and enriching of the bonds of Christian worship and fellowship. To meet this need the church must provide an adequate Music Ministry and opportunities for the people to be together in Christian social and recreational activities. Indeed, all areas of the Christian's life—home, business, school, play—should be made to feel the interest and the guidance of the church's ministry.

There is a need for help in the crises of life and in all the great experiences that come in the course of a lifetime. At the time of birth or marriage, tragedy or sorrow, the church should be ready to step in and minister to those in need. This is a time of unparalleled opportunity for spiritual growth and understanding which we dare not miss. We are to be custodian of the crises of life.

The areas mentioned are by no means exhaustive but they, at least, point the way in which our churches can go to help its members grow into mature Christians. We should never become static either as individuals or as a church. If the members of the church continue to grow, the church should also continue to grow. No program should be accepted as final. The church should ever be seeking new and better ways to meet the needs of its people!

"The Church itself must grow. It must become mature in mind and spirit. It must not be choked by tradition, and it dare not become a servant of modern culture. There are childish churches just as there are childish Christians. Both must forget those things which are behind, and reach toward those things which are before . . . Above all, the secret of growth in the Church is in its constant exposure to the source and succor of its existence, the gospel of Jesus Christ, in the light of which it is both judged on its defects and faults and saved by self-criticism and obedient trust." [6]

3. *The Church Can Help Each Member Keep in Touch with the Source of Life*

It would be difficult to place one area of service above another that the church gives to the new Christian. That which is perhaps more important because it is more inclusive than all the others in worship. "The late Archbishop Temple used to urge that the world can be saved only by worship. He did not mean that the world's salvation depends upon the maintenance of the forms of worship. He meant by worship recognition of and response to the sovereignty and grace of God. So construed, it is beyond dispute that the worship of God has priority rights over the service of men. It is the first and central duty of the Church." [7]

Worship includes meditation on God's word, prayer, praise, proclamation of the gospel, dedication. In fact, it involves the giving of our total selves to the glorifying of God. It brings us into fellowship with others in an experience of corporate worship, but it is also an experience which we can and must have personally. It clarifies our sense of values. It makes us aware of our own sinfulness and unworthiness. It keeps us sensitive to our holy God and his will. It sends us forth to dedicated living. No matter how good the programs of our churches are, they are not good enough to keep us growing spiritually if we lose vital touch with the Source of our life. Your church calls you to worship. It should provide the means for this sublime encounter with God.

IV. WHAT WE CAN MEAN TO THE CHURCH

We have been thinking about what the church can mean to us—what the church owes us. It does have a God-given responsibility to those who become a part of its life. This, however, is not a one-way street. Sometimes we get the impression that we have come to look at all life from this point of view—what it owes me. The home, the school, the employer, the state—indeed, the world owes me a living!

Let's look at the other side. What can I mean to my church —what do I owe it? Jesus "loved the church and gave himself for it." If we love him because of what he has done for us and his church for what it means to us we should delight in serving him through his church. We should give ourselves in loyal, unselfish devotion to it.

1. *We Should Be Grateful for Its Heritage*

Arnold Toynbee, the eminent historian, has called the Christian church the "carrier of culture" from the classical civilization of the Mediterranean to the new civilization of Europe and eventually America. Another has said that ". . . it is the moral and spiritual heritage of the Hebrew-Christian tradition. This is the seedbed of the great ideas of democracy, freedom and justice. Wherever this religious tradition has gone, these ideas have sprung up." It is a well known fact that the "blood of the martyrs became the seed of the church." [8]

However we view it, the church has brought to us and our children untold riches. Above all, it has carried to us the "unsearchable riches of the gospel of Jesus Christ." But for the movement of the church westward under the guidance of God's spirit we today might constitute the pagan world.

Furthermore, the Christian faith in general and our Baptist interpretation in particular have been carried to us by those who have suffered banishment, persecution, ridicule, imprisonment and even death for their faith in the gospel and the freedom to proclaim it.

No one would claim that the church has always been true to its Lord and his way, but if there is any doubt about its place in our society, strip your community of its churches and their influence and see what life would be without them. Yes, we can thank God for the church and that it has come to our land.

2. *We Can Stand for Its Faith*

There are those who have the impression that the church only speaks when it is against something. Perhaps, with good reason. There are times when we must be against some things but, if we are, let them not be insignificant trifles. If we are against something, let it be because we stand for something that is tremendous.

When Jesus said, "It is on this rock that I am going to found my Church, and the powers of death will never prevail against it" (Matt. 16:18, Phillips), he was not talking about the church on the defensive. He was talking about the church storming the battlements of hell. It was so because he had found a man—or he would find many men down the ages— who believed that he was the Son of God.

As Christians and as Baptists there are some great affirmations of faith for which we stand. They are the absolute lordship and authority of Jesus Christ, the New Testament as the only and all-sufficient rule of faith and practice, the competency of the individual soul in religion, the priesthood of every believer, an experience of grace with Jesus Christ as the only means of salvation, the independence and autonomy of the church, the symbolism of baptism and the Lord's Supper, and the separation of church and state—a free church in a free state.

As members of our church we will stand tall as Christians and think and live positively in our community if we stand on these and other great tenets of the faith that is ours in Christ.

3. *We Can Share in Its Responsibility*

The church deserves our gratitude; it merits our devotion to its great doctrines, but it has a tremendous assignment. It is to carry the witness and ministry of Christ to the whole world—beginning where you are. Missions is not a special function of a part of the church. It is the whole church in action. It is the body of Christ expressing Christ's concern for the whole world. It is God's people seeking to make all men members of the people of God. Missions is the function for which the church exists.

In that assignment the church needs the help of every member. Our great question should not be "What can the church do for me?" but, "What can I do for Christ through his church?"

We can *pray* for our church. And this is not something we do because we can't do anything else. It was when all the people were together and prayed on the eve of Pentecost that the church went rolling across the pagan world like a prairie fire—out of control. Pray for your pastor. Pray for your leadership. Pray during the services. Pray through the week. Prayer can make the difference between a weak, vascillating, divided congregation and a dynamic body in action for Christ.

We can *give*. "Know ye not that . . . ye are not your own? For ye are bought with a price" (1 Cor. 6:19-20). The theology of Christian stewardship is based on the ownership of God—"The earth is the Lord's"—and the Lordship of Christ. When we accept that we do not lose ourselves in the "petty calculating of more or less." It is all his. The tithe and more becomes a means of acknowledging his lordship through our church. For the sake of its worldwide ministry it needs all you can possibly give. We do not honor Christ with any less.

We can *serve*. The Christian who has had a genuine experience with Jesus Christ will feel such a sense of love and gratitude that he will begin to seek means by which he, in turn, can help others. He must not stifle that impulse. He must not be content to listen and learn and receive. He must find some place of service commensurate with his talent.

The church offers all of us many opportunities. Discover the thing you enjoy doing. Find the age group you like to work with or are effective in leading. Place your talents at the disposal of your church, and the door of opportunity will open. Then, by all means, be willing to "Study to shew thyself approved unto God, a workman that needeth not to be ashamed, rightly dividing the word of truth" (2 Tim. 2:15).

Finally, we can let our *influence* count for our church. How many people have taken a second look at the church simply because some faithful member "never missed a service." Loyalty is not the only measure of one's devotion to his home or his country or his church, but can you name a better one? There are those who, in the economy of providence, have little else to give, but they give that! "Not forsaking the assembling of ourselves together, as the manner of some is; but exhorting one another: and so much the more, as ye see the day approaching" (Heb. 10:25). They take that seriously.

But beyond the walls of the church building, beyond the faithfulness in attendance, a man's influence should count for Christ. How many have stayed out of the church because of the "poor quality" of Christian living on the part of those who were members!

The followers of Christ, we are told, were first called *Christians* in Antioch (Acts 11:26). Could it be because there had come to Antioch one by the name of Barnabas of whom it was said, "He was a good man, and full of the Holy Ghost and of faith" (Acts 11:24). There is no telling how far the influence of a "good man" will go. The church needs many such men— those who will bring Christian living into the halls of government, the councils of business, and the front room of life. The church needs your influence, and the world needs it even more.

There is a new awareness in our day of the importance of the church in the minds of Christian leaders and in the life of the world. Many are giving serious thought to understanding its meaning and its mission. "In C. S. Lewis' *Screwtape Letters* the Devil in hell is giving advice to one of his agents on the earth assigned to keep a man from becoming a real Christian. The intended victim has joined the church and has the Devil's agent worried. But Screwtape gives this assurance: 'There is no need to despair' (if the victim does not see the Church itself) 'as we see her spread out through time and space and rooted in eternity, terrible as an army with banners. That, I confess, is a spectacle which makes our boldest tempters uneasy.' It is hard to imagine truer words put into more vivid picture: the Christian Church with all her banners flying striking fear into the heart of hell." [9]

FOR FURTHER STUDY AND DISCUSSION

1. Some books that will help stimulate discussion on the nature and mission of the church—perhaps not always from our point of view are: *The Glory of God in the Christian Calling*, W. O. Carver; *The Church Militant*, Harold Bosley; *The Nature and Mission of the Church*, Donald Miller
2. Take time to look up some of the references in the New Testament that have to do with "the church." Determine whether or not they refer to the local body or to the larger fellowship.
3. Discuss some of the contributions that the church has made to Western civilization and to your own community—both good and bad.
4. Secure helps for new church members from the Sunday School Board and set up a suggested program that your church may use in helping new Christians become effective church members.

CHAPTER 6 OUTLINE

I. THE NATURE OF GOD'S KINGDOM

   1. The Background of God's Kingdom

   2. The Message of God's Kingdom

   3. The Meaning of God's Kingdom

II. THE CITIZEN OF GOD'S KINGDOM

   1. His Character

   2. His Influence

   3. His Conduct

   4. His Destiny

III. THE DEVELOPMENT OF GOD'S KINGDOM

   1. How It Grows

   2. The Continuing Tension

   3. The Final Victory

6

God's Kingdom on Earth—
the New Citizen

MAN LIVES in two worlds. He lives in a world whose dimensions can be measured. It has breadth and length. It knows the boundaries of time and space. Its substance is material. He lives also in a spiritual world. It has dimensions in depth— love and faith and hope. They cannot be measured or weighed. They are not limited by time or space. They are one with eternity.

Now in the same sense the Christian is a citizen of two kingdoms. Paul was a Jew. He was a member of the Jewish nation. He was also a Roman citizen. But when Paul accepted Christ he became a citizen of the kingdom of God. When he wrote to the Christians in Philippi he knew he was writing to people who were a part of the Roman Empire—a kingdom in time which was subject to decay. He refers to the Christians, however, as citizens of "the colony of heaven." He sets the two in vivid contrast with each other. Of the one he says, "Their end is destruction, their god is the belly, and they glory in their shame, with minds set on earthly things" (Phil. 3:19, RSV). Of the other he says, "But our commonwealth is in heaven, and from it we await a Savior, the Lord Jesus Christ" (Phil. 3:20, RSV).

When we accept Christ as Saviour we become a citizen in his kingdom. As such we enjoy incomparable privileges. Those privileges demand great responsibilities. Our supreme allegiance is to Jesus Christ, the king of this kingdom.

No discussion of the new life in Christ would be complete without including in it the Christian's place in this larger fellowship that crosses all national, racial, social, and economic barriers—the kingdom of God.

I. THE NATURE OF GOD'S KINGDOM

Every great leader, every movement that has dominated and changed the life of the world has been mastered by some central, all-controlling idea. It was true of Islam, democracy, communism—of Mohammed, Jefferson, Lenin.

No one would question that the idea of "the kingdom of God" was the dominant idea, the magnificent obsession of Jesus Christ. Says Dr. James Stewart, "Every great leader who has towered up above the sons of men has had some one thought that held and haunted and dominated him, one thought that drove a passage for him through this close-grained earth and lifted him high. Now the greatest leader who has ever led the hosts of humanity is Jesus Christ. And Jesus, like all these others, came with his master-thought, glorious and thrilling, world-shaking and world-transforming, and Christ's master-thought was 'the Kingdom of God.'" [1]

In one form or another—"the kingdom of heaven," "the kingdom of God," or simply, "the kingdom" is the term most frequently on his lips. It holds a central place in his teachings and in his life. It was the subject of his first sermon: "The time is fulfilled, and the kingdom of God is at hand" (Mark 1:15). His greatest recorded sermon, the Sermon on the Mount, has been called "the manifesto of the kingdom of God." It was his concern in his final message as he spoke to his disciples of "the kingdom of God" (Acts 1:3).

Why was this idea so everlastingly important to Jesus? What did he mean by it? What was the nature of his kingdom?

1. *The Background of God's Kingdom*

The coming of the kingdom of God was not the coming of a new and loftier ethic; nor was it the introduction of a new theology; nor was it the beginning of a new religion.

When Jesus announced the idea of the kingdom of God he was talking about an idea that was familiar to the people of Israel. Dr. John Bright in his comprehensive study, *The Kingdom of God,* establishes beyond any doubt that the idea had its roots in the faith and hope of the Old Testament. In summary he says: "We have, up to this point, followed through the Old Testament a single theme, that of the people of God. We have traced it from its roots in the Mosaic faith; we have seen how it was given shape by the blows of history and by prophet word; we have followed it until we saw it solidify into the beliefs and practices of Judaism. We have seen that there always accompanied it the concomitant hope of the consummation of God's purpose and the establishment of his Kingdom. Although this hope took many and various forms, it was always one hope. And although it was many times cruelly frustrated, it was never given up. It was never given up, because it was in the very texture of Israel's faith—indeed at the core of that faith—and to have surrendered it would have been to surrender faith itself. As long as Israel retained any sense of calling as the people of God, or any faith in the integrity and power of that God who is Lord of history, so long would there live the lively expectation of his coming Kingdom." [2]

Although their views of the coming king and the kingdom were distorted, as is evidenced by their reception, yet, their Messianic hopes were tied together—the coming of the Messiah and the establishment of his kingdom.

In the generation prior to the coming of Jesus two factors had a noticeable bearing upon the Jewish idea of the coming kingdom. For one thing the expectancy was intensified because of the domination of the power of Rome over Israel. They longed for one whose power could deliver them from the hated power of their oppressor. The other factor involved the almost complete secularization of the idea of the kingdom. The kingdoms they knew were characterized by material splendours, political powers, secular benefits. It was inevitable that this would be the nature of the kingdom they hoped for. It was this strong feeling of nationalism and materialism that brought the Jewish leaders as well as the populace into such bitter conflict with Jesus when they learned the truth—he was not that kind of a king and his kingdom was not to their liking. Even his disciples found it exceedingly difficult to break with these prevailing ideas and as late as his post-resurrection appearance before Pentecost they were saying, "Lord, wilt thou at this time restore again the kingdom to Israel?" (Acts 1:6).

Considering this strong feeling of expectancy, we are not surprised, then, that when John came preaching in the wilderness the good news of the kingdom the people flocked to hear him. Likewise, Jesus' message was received at first with popular acclaim. It remained for him to interpret to them the real meaning of the kingdom of God and to enlist them to become citizens in it.

2. The Message of God's Kingdom

If the idea of the kingdom of God was as old as the dreams of the children of Israel, then was there anything new about Christ's dramatic announcement? Exactly wherein was the good news of his kingdom?

We have noted that he did not come to introduce a new ethic or a new theology or a new religion. He did not come to destroy the religion of his fathers. And it soon became apparent that he did not come to destroy the government of Rome!

This was his terse, dramatic proclamation: *"The time is fulfilled, and the kingdom of God is at hand: repent ye, and believe the gospel"* (Mark 1:15). That is to say, "This is what you have been waiting for. The God of old, your God, has now acted. This is the fulfilment of your long expectancy.

The Messiah is now here. God has come to do what he has long promised if you will accept him—on his terms."

We know now in retrospect and some of them would know that Christ himself was the good news. The hope, not only of Israel, but of the whole world had become a present fact in Jesus Christ. In the person and work of Jesus the kingdom of God has intruded into the world.

Christ, then, had come to establish his kingdom among men and was calling them to accept. His mission was not simply to instruct men in a better way of life, to impart to them a clearer understanding of God, to attack the faults of the Jewish law or the governments and abuses of established political and social orders, although all of this happened as a result of his coming. He came to call men with a tremendous urgency to make a radical decision for him and his kingdom. Nothing less than the experience that would be like a new birth would do. Men must "repent and believe." They must pledge their supreme allegiance to the King of the kingdom!

3. *The Meaning of God's Kingdom*

If the kingdom of God was not to be a political kingdom— like the kingdom of David—or, if its purpose was not primarily to bring material benefits, then what was it? What was the meaning of the kingdom as Jesus conceived it?

For his church Jesus used a term, "ecclesia," patterned after the Greek assembly. For his kingdom he borrows an idea from the Roman Empire, "basilea," giving it a wider more universal content. In other words, the predominant idea of the church is the visible, assembled unit within the larger fellowship of the kingdom.

Actually and specifically, the kingdom of God means *the reign or rule of God in the lives of men.* Although it was not to have earth-bound dimensions, geographical frontiers, or so many square miles—it was no empty domain. It was to be made up of people. Christ came to lay claim to the lives of people. He called men to accept his kingship. Those who obeyed would constitute his kingdom.

Where would that reign begin? It would begin in the hearts of individuals. Jesus did not come to attempt a sweeping reform by changing political and social conditions; he came to change men from within. He spoke to men's inner thoughts and motives. Jesus said, "The kingdom of God cometh not with observation: Neither shall they say, Lo here! or, lo there! for, behold, the kingdom of God is within you" (Luke 17:20–21).

Dr. James Stewart makes these three interesting observations concerning the rule of Christ in the heart. First, the kingdom of God is moral, not nationalistic. That is to say, the true enemy of man is not some outward political tyrant but man's moral enemy within his own heart. It was against this evil that Jesus directed his attack. Second, the kingdom of God is spiritual, not material. Those of Jesus' day—both Gentile and Jew—had set their hearts on the good things of material life. The power of earthly kingdom, the benefits of the material world dominated their lives. Jesus called man to seek "first the kingdom of God, and his righteousness" (Matt. 6:33). Third, the kingdom of God was actual, not ideal. Many of the Jews had projected their dreams of the kingdom as something that belonged to the future. They were not prepared to accept it as a present reality. Jesus came to say, "It is here now; it is at hand."

It follows, however, that the rule of God cannot be confined to the individual life. Christ's reign must extend through individuals to every area of life. It is the rule of God in the heart, but it is also the rule of God in the world. God's sovereign reign must at last encompass the whole creation of things and men.

Again we turn to Dr. Stewart's clear distinction in this area. First, the kingdom of God is social, not individualistic. If

Christ rules in a man's heart it follows that Christ's will must be carried out in all his social relationships and responsibilities. If he loves God in his heart he should also love those who need him.

Second, the kingdom of God is universal, not local. If anything is clear in the claims of Christ it is that every citizen in his kingdom has a world responsibility. "The field is the world," he said. One of the great surprises, to those with a provincial point of view would be that, "They shall come from the east, and from the west, and from the north, and from the south, and shall sit down in the kingdom of God" (Luke 13 : 29).

Third, the kingdom of God awaits final consummation; it is not yet complete. At the heart of the prayer that Jesus taught his disciples is this dominant desire, "Thy kingdom come. Thy will be done in earth, as it is in heaven" (Matt. 6 : 10). That is the goal; that is the ideal. It is obvious to all, however, that that ideal is far from a reality. Christ came to reign in the hearts of men and in the world, and Christ must and will, at last, reign. That is the meaning and ultimate purpose of his kingdom. The dream has not yet come true.

II. The Citizen of God's Kingdom

We come now to consider more specifically those who belong to Christ's kingdom—their character, their influence, their conduct, and their destiny. Embodied in his great discourse at the beginning of his ministry are these qualities. We must keep in mind that the Sermon on the Mount was not given as a way of life that would lead men to Christ or as a grand ethic to be lived apart from Christ. Superb as it is in its moral principles and spiritual insights, that was not its intent.

It was given to his disciples and for his disciples. Men could not understand, much less follow, its high precepts unless they had been "born from above." Jesus is not here painting a picture of a man as he must be to become a citizen of his kingdom, but rather, the portrait of the person who is to be the result of his life, work, and death. Christ has come to make this ideal man a reality. He cannot even begin unless he begins with Christ. He gives not a set of rules to be kept but a design for living for those who have trusted him as Saviour and would follow him as Lord.

1. *His Character*

Said an elderly man as he studied carefully the son of an old friend whom he was meeting for the first time, "I just wanted to see if there was any of your father's likeness in you!"

In that portion of the sermon called the Beatitudes Jesus sets forth those qualities of life which should characterize the Christian. Indeed, they are qualities of the Father revealed in his Son Jesus Christ. These are the qualities so evident in the Master's life. They constitute the ideal for us. They describe the aspects of mature citizens of Christ's kingdom. What are they?

First, we are to approach the whole matter of Christian learning and living in the spirit of humility and acknowledgment of our spiritual poverty and need. We stand empty-handed before God. "Blessed are the poor in spirit" (Matt. 5:3).

Second, we recognize our true spiritual condition as sinners. We come deeply dissatisfied with ourselves, knowing that no man can find peace who has made peace with sin. There must be genuine sorrow for sin. "Blessed are they that mourn" (Matt. 5:4).

Third, we know that in Christ's kingdom we gain by losing. Meekness is not a sign of weakness; it is a sign of our dependence upon God and our willingness to obey his will. "Blessed are the meek" (Matt. 5:5).

Fourth, a man's life moves ever in the direction of his dominant desire—not what he says he wants but what he really wants. The desire of the Christian, uttered or unexpressed, should be the righteousness of God. "Blessed are they which do hunger and thirst after righteousness" (Matt. 5:6).

Fifth, we know that God's mercy springs not out of cheap sentiment but from compassionate holiness. Ever indebted to him for his mercy, we too shall be merciful. "Blessed are the merciful" (Matt. 5:7).

Sixth, purity here means not moral perfection but singleness of heart—devotion without alloy. The Christian has only one Master. He has an eye single to the Lord's will and service. "Blessed are the pure in heart" (Matt. 5:8).

Seventh, God's greatest work was that of reconciliation. "God was in Christ, reconciling the world unto himself" (2 Cor. 5:19). That, too, should be our greatest work. Nonviolence is not enough; love must take the initiative. "Blessed are the peacemakers" (Matt. 5:9).

These are the characteristics of a kingdom man. Beginning with the recognition of his spiritual poverty and his inability to supply the need, he develops until he becomes a useful citizen in God's kingdom.

To the degree that we live up to the qualities of a kingdom man we bear the characteristics of our Lord. To the degree that they characterize our thoughts and deeds we find true happiness and inward peace.

2. *His Influence*

What a man is is reflected in what he does. Such lives as those described in the Beatitudes will make their impact upon the world. Their influence will be felt in so far as they remain true to their character.

What a compliment and what a responsibility Jesus thrust upon his followers when he called them, "the salt of the earth" and "the light of the world." Few common, every day elements could be more descriptive of the influence that a

Christian can have upon society. What does he say about us when he calls us "salt?" It does not call attention to itself. By its very quality it improves that of which it is a part. It banishes life's insipidness and adds zest and taste to living. It preserves that which is good and checks the creeping putrefaction of evil influences. How easily is good society corrupted by lust, selfishness, greed. Without the presence of the counteracting influence of Christians, God only knows how bad the world might become. Jesus adds this sobering thought. Salt can lose its saltiness. When the purpose for which it was intended is lost it is good for nothing!

So, too, he says our influence is like light. Only light can reveal. Without it all is swallowed up in darkness. Only light can dispel the darkness. There is not enough darkness in the world to put out the light of one small candle! Without light there can be no life. And the life that we have is from him who is the light of the world. The light that we bear is the light of his reflected glory. "Your light" is the light that you are, not any light you may hold. As Christians, we are to be examples, not to set them. We are to shine where we are placed with the light that we are. A city set on a hill cannot be hid. We are to shine like something that cannot be hid. Men do not light a lamp and put it under a bushel, but on a lampstand. The lamp is placed by another. We are lighted and placed for God's purposes.

3. *His Conduct*

Any discussion of the conduct of the citizens of the kingdom must of necessity be limited. All we can hope to do is to call attention to some of the principles which Jesus sets forth in his Sermon on the Mount. For that is what he did. He did not give a set of specific rules to be followed, but he laid down moral principles that are to serve as guides in any situation in every age.

In the first place, the conduct of the Christian must be

characterized by a superior brand of righteousness. The average, decent, accepted standard is not enough. Jesus said, "For I tell you, unless your righteousness exceeds that of the scribes and Pharisees, you will never enter the kingdom of heaven" (Matt. 5:20, RSV). That is to say that the Christian must go beyond the norm, putting the extra quality into life. It must include the inward thought as well as the outward expression. This principle is to apply to every area of life.

In the second place, the Christian must give attention to the motive of his conduct. The end does not justify the means. This applies to the giving of alms or praying or religious activity. Jesus said, "Beware of practicing your piety before men in order to be seen by them; for then you will have no reward from your Father who is in heaven" (Matt. 6:1, RSV). We need to look to our motives.

Furthermore, the Christian must learn how properly to weigh the values of life. What comes first? What is of greatest value—food, clothing, self-satisfaction? Jesus said that where the treasure was—that which was deemed to be of greatest value—there would be also the center of life's devotion. He said, "Do not lay up for yourselves treasures on earth, where moth and rust consume and where thieves break in and steal. . . . For where your treasure is, there will your heart be also" (Matt. 6:19–21, RSV). And again, "But seek first his kingdom and his righteousness, and all these things shall be yours as well" (Matt. 6:33, RSV).

Finally, the Christian's conduct must be governed by moral discernment. He must see others as God sees them. He must treat others as he would want them to treat him. Consequently, he is not to pass unjust judgment upon others because by the standards he judges, he will be judged. For the Christian the golden rule is a working principle of life; for the non-Christian it is impossible. Says one, "Whatsoever ye would that men should do to you if you were in their place. Such is the clear implication. If you were a clerk in a department store, or a Negro, or a man in jail, how would you wish to be treated? So the rule, having first required purest conscience, now requires ultimate love. It asks complete understanding and sympathy: 'if you were in his place.' " [3] We need ever to judge with moral and spiritual insight, to look at life through God's eyes.

4. His Destiny

Jesus closes his sermon with a high call to man's destiny. What that destiny shall be depends upon what his decision is, upon what he really is—and there can be no make-believe. Life's destiny can be traced to its choices—there is the low way and the high, the narrow way and the broad, the easy way and the way of discipline—and every man must decide which way he shall go. Jesus said, "Enter by the narrow gate; for the gate is wide and the way is easy, that leads to destruction, and those who enter by it are many. For the gate is narrow and the way is hard, that leads to life, and those who find it are few" (Matt. 7:13–14, RSV).

Man's destiny would be revealed by what a man was, not by what he said he was. His profession must be validated by his performance. "You will know them by their fruits. Are grapes gathered from thorns, or figs from thistles? . . . Every tree that does not bear good fruit is cut down and thrown into the fire. . . . Not every one who says to me, 'Lord, Lord,' shall enter the kingdom of heaven, but he who does the will of my Father who is in heaven" (Matt. 7:16–21, RSV).

Man's destiny would be determined by the foundation on which he would build his life. Here again we cannot fool Christ. We may not be able to take him literally, but we must take him seriously! "Every one then who hears these words of mine and does them will be like a wise man who built his house upon the rock; and the rain fell, and the floods came, and the winds blew and beat upon that house, but it did not fall, because it had been founded on the rock. And every one who hears these words of mine and does not do them will be like a foolish man who built his house upon the sand; and the rain fell, and the floods came, and the winds blew and beat against that house, and it fell; and great was the fall of it" (Matt. 7:24–27, RSV). Jesus' words afford the only secure foundation for time or eternity. Note that it is Jesus' words which afford security, and that they afford security only as men hear and obey. Belief that Christ is the Saviour does not afford a safe foundation for this life or the next, unless it includes loyal submission to him as Lord. Professions are of no avail unless one does the will of God.

III. THE DEVELOPMENT OF GOD'S KINGDOM

How shall we think of the development of God's kingdom? It had its roots in the life of God's people long before the time of Christ. Christ announced its intrusion into history with his coming: "The kingdom of God is at hand." It now stretches over almost two thousand years. His rule, to some degree, at least, has been felt in the hearts and lives of people of every nation and race. But has his kingdom come; is it now coming; or, is it yet to come?

Although allowance must be made for a wide difference of opinion on the "how" and "when" of his coming kingdom, we believe that Jesus' teachings must include a positive answer to all three questions. His kingdom has come; it is coming; it is yet to come.

1. *How It Grows*

Earlier in this chapter we dealt with Jesus' dramatic proclamation that the kingdom was a present reality. It was at hand, and men were being summoned to repent and believe. They were soon to see that it was not to be a kingdom identified with any political or social order. It was not to have geographical boundaries. Its primary purpose was not to bring material benefits. During the last days of his life Jesus said to Pilate, "My kingdom is not of this world: if my kingdom were of this world, then would my servants fight, that I should not be delivered to the Jews: but now is my kingdom not from hence" (John 18:36). That is to say, it is not a man-made kingdom; it is not run according to the principles of world kingdoms. It is heaven-sent. It is a spiritual kingdom.

When this became clear to many who had been following him they were deeply disappointed. They saw no future in the kingdom that he envisioned. They turned back and followed him no more. This was neither the king nor the kingdom they wanted!

Well, what was the future for his kingdom? How was it to grow? In a number of his kingdom parables Jesus seeks to bring encouragement and hope to his followers. Its growth will be in the framework of this evil world. The good and the evil for the time at least, must grow together (Matt. 13:24–30). He indicates that the sowing of the seed must be in the world field. The sower is a noble prodigal, broadcasting his seed everywhere—not knowing where it will take root and grow (Matt. 13:3–9).

In two of his parables he illustrates the how of its growth. "The kingdom of heaven is like to a grain of mustard seed," he said. And again, "The kingdom of heaven is like unto leaven" (Matt. 13:31, 33). Says Dr. Conner, "Starting from insignificant beginnings it is to become a mighty worldwide power. Some say that the parable of the leaven represents the leavening power of Christianity in the individual life, while the parable of the mustard seed teaches the spread of Christianity in the world at large. Whether this is true or not, it is true that Jesus meant to show that Christianity was to have a growth indefinitely great in the world. Just how great is to be the development no one can tell. Evidently the kingdom of God is to become a mighty power in the world's life." [4]

Always and ever it is to grow by God's grace and under his care, as the lily of the field grows. Man is needed to sow, to cultivate, to water, but it is God who gives the increase. Yes, there is a future to God's kingdom. There is a time of harvest coming. His kingdom's goal has not been realized, but God's eternal purpose is being worked out.

2. *The Continuing Tension*

Man is destined to live out his life in the struggle between the ideal and the reality. Christ's kingdom has not come, and yet man is urged to become a citizen of the kingdom. He is asked to be perfect as the Father in heaven is perfect, and yet he knows that is not possible. Jesus taught his disciples— and us—to pray, "Thy kingdom come. Thy will be done in earth, as it is in heaven," knowing that he was urging us to ask for that which must ever remain above and beyond us.

That, of course, is the paradox of his kingdom and of our Christian faith. Writes Dr. Bright: "Therein lie the seeds of extreme tension. For it was equally clear, that the Kingdom had not come and its victory had not been won nor, from a human point of view, was there any way to produce that victory. That is indeed paradox! What is the Kingdom that has come but has not come, that is already victorious but is anything but victorious?" [5]

It takes no prophetic insight to see that his kingdom has not come, his will is not being done in our individual lives, much less in the world at large. Instead of a steady, upward climb toward progressive righteousness we have seen, in our day, mankind retrogress to the darkest possible abyss of conduct. Any hope that the world is getting better "day by day in every way" is sheer foolishness. Evil is still with us. But remember, so also is the kingdom of God and the power that its King has released in the world.

The kingdom of God has come and is even now in the world. It is also yet to come. The ideal has not been realized.

In the tension between the two we must live and do our work. "The New Testament church stood in a peculiar mid-position between what had been done and what was awaited, between the present age which was dying and the new age struggling to be born. It was confident that the victory over all the dark powers of the old aeon had been won in Christ, so much so that the Kingdom of God could be spoken of as a present thing. Yet it was all too painfully aware that that Kingdom remained an unconsummated thing of the future which had yet to come in its power. In tension between the two the New Testament church lived and waited. It was a tension between the victory and the victory anything but won, between the Kingdom which is at hand and the Kingdom unseen and unrealized, between the power of God and the power of Caesar, between the church militant and suffering and the church triumphant." [6]

3. *The Final Victory*

When and how will his kingdom finally come? The "when" and the "how" we shall not attempt to answer. Of the "when" it is given to no man to know. This was Jesus' clear affirmation. As to the exact method of that consummation, there is a difference of opinion.

Here we elect to point only to the certainty of the victory. What God began in Christ and is now carrying forward he will complete. "The Kingdom of God, then, is a power already released in the world. True, its beginnings are tiny, and it might seem incredible that the humble ministry of this obscure Galilean could be the dawning of the new age of God. Yet it is! What has been begun here will surely go on to its conclusion; nothing can stop it. And the conclusion is victory. Over and over again this motif recurs in the teachings of Jesus . . . It is small now, but in these small beginnings there lie hidden its victory. And that victory will reach out into all the earth, for 'all authority . . . has been given to me' (Matt. 28:18)." [7]

His victory is not to be identified with any political philosophy or social or economic way of life. His kingdom comes not with observation, nor is the arch enemy to be identified with any particular person of history. How many men have been made the antichrist! It is rather all earthly powers that are subservient to the adversary. Christ's victory must be at last victory over him and the areas of life where he holds sway.

Jesus did not seem to expect victory within history. It would take the form of no victorious nation in the scheme of history as we know it. His coming would not initiate the kingdom but consummate it. His victory would be above and beyond victory. Toward that far-off divine event the whole creation moves. That victory can come only with his coming. Then and only then will the dream be realized: "The kingdoms of this world are become the kingdoms of our Lord, and of his Christ; and he shall reign for ever and ever" (Rev. 11:15).

FOR FURTHER STUDY AND DISCUSSION

1. If the kingdom of God was meant to be a pattern of conduct for today, in what ways would life be different for us as individuals and in all of our social relationships if we would let Christ truly reign?
2. The Sermon on the Mount may be used as a basis for a more careful study and discussion of the manifesto of Christ's kingdom.
3. Since many of the parables of Jesus are related to the teachings of his kingdom, they could be used as a basis for discussion. Several excellent books on the parables of the kingdom are available.
4. Discuss the various views held concerning the consummation or final victory for Christ's kingdom.

CHAPTER 7 OUTLINE

I. THE WORLD URGENCY
1. The Lost World
2. The Lost Provinces
3. The Lost Potential

II. THE USE OF OUR LIVES
1. Being Our Best Selves
2. Our Money and Our Lives
3. Using All That We Have

III. THAT MAN MAY KNOW
1. The World Challenge
2. Every Christian's Job
3. Unto the Uttermost

7

Living with a Sense of Divine Mission—
the New Vocation

WHAT SHALL WE DO with our lives? What use shall we make of them? These are decisive questions for all of us. It may be the question of a restless teen-ager. He does not know what to do with himself. He has life on his hands, and he does not know how to use it.

That is a part of the growing youth. We trust that he will find himself. It becomes increasingly tragic if one comes to maturity and still does not know what to do with his life. Now a grown man, he still has no sense of purpose. He lives under the shadow of meaningless boredom. At last he reaches the age of retirement. How will he use the remaining years of his life? He may well come to the end with a feeling of frustration. He had the gift of life but to what end?

The answers he finds to these searching questions will largely determine his personal happiness, his usefulness to society, and the direction his life goes—today and for a lifetime. We have only one life to live. But we do have one life, and we should determine to make it count for something eternally worthwhile.

When we became Christians—new creatures in Christ—we came into possession of a new life. We were changed. We looked at all of life from a new point of view. It should have brought also a new purpose for living. We should come to see that not only does all the world belong to God, but we belong to him. We owe our very life to Christ. As Paul said: "You are not your own; you were bought with a price" (1 Cor. 6:19-20, RSV). Our life should become his life. Our purpose

101

should become his purpose. We should seek to find our place in his redemptive mission—the making of a new humanity.

I. The World Urgency

The all-encompassing mission which brought Christ into this world scheme of things is set forth in these familiar lines: "For God so loved the world, that he gave his only begotten Son, that whosoever believeth in him should not perish, but have everlasting life. For God sent not his Son into the world to condemn the world; but that the world through him might be saved" (John 3:16–17). That not only sets the bounds of God's saving mission; it also points up the urgency for it. The world is a lost, dying world.

1. *The Lost World*

In what sense is his created world lost? Only in the sense that man has usurped God's right to dominion. Only because man has taken over that which rightfully belongs to God and is using it for his own purposes. The world is lost because man is lost. He willed to go against God's intent. He missed the mark—the goal of God. "For all have sinned, and come short of the glory of God" (Rom. 3:23).

So it is man that is lost. All men are lost. They are lost in their ignorance or blindness or rebellion against God. They urgently, desperately need a Saviour. That is true of all men. It is true of each man. Once a man went into the great Mojave Desert during his vacation to spend a night all alone. While he was making preparations to settle for the night an old man drove out of the darkness, stopped his car, and called to him: "Are you lost?" The man replied, "No, just came out to camp." "That's fine," called the old man, "just thought I'd ask. This desert is an awful place to get lost in!" This world is an awful place to get lost in. So tragic is man's lostness, so urgent is his need to be saved that God gave his Son—in suffering and death—that man might find his way.

2. *The Lost Provinces*

Not only did that lostness encompass the whole world of man—and that with each recurring generation, for each generation is a lost generation—it also involved the whole man.

One of the tragedies of our day or any day is that we conceive man as saved by fragments. His soul is saved—whatever we may mean by that—but what of his mind? He is saved for eternity, but what about being saved "in time"?

Elton Trueblood gives us that strikingly descriptive phrase *"lost provinces."* He says: "Our strategy is to find new areas into which the fundamental Christian insights can penetrate and thus change the world. There is no good reason why the words of the risen Lord, 'Go, ye, into all the world,' may not be taken *intensively* as well as *extensively*. Usually we have interpreted this injunction in a geographical sense, but there is a deeper significance, according to which they may mean that all phases of life, economic, political, cultural and domestic, must be deeply penetrated. If our new order is to succeed in the recovery of the lost provinces it must be a society of penetrators in common life, not people separated from it." [1]

Because man has not been totally committed to Jesus Christ great areas of his society and culture go unclaimed. Although there are some outstanding philanthropists among the wealthy classes, for the most part these vast resources remain undedicated to the purpose of Christ.

Or, take that ever-increasing powerful class in American society—organized labor. Here again we must point out that a few of their leaders are responsible Christian men, but for the most part this organization pays little attention to the church. That is said without seeking to lay the blame either on organized labor or the church. It is simply to observe a fact—here is a great and growing lost province!

Another area is that of education. Education that received its initial impetus from the Christian movement is more and more becoming secularized. The intellectual leaders of our society have not to any serious degree included Christ in their thinking. Our schools are not designed to teach us to love God with "all of our minds."

Wealth, labor, education—these we have singled out as lost provinces. There are others we could mention. As the leader of one great American industry boldly put it and as we have said in essence before, "We need faith to bring God into the councils of business, the halls of government, and the front room of life." Indeed, we shall not be able to save the world until we begin making inroads for Christ into some of these areas.

3. *The Lost Potential*

When Christ came to save the world he came to save the whole world—that is, man on every geographical frontier. As we have just said, he also came to save man in his total relationship, in all the areas of his life. He also came to save the total man to the inclusion of his potential. He claims each man and all men for what they are now and also for what they can be. Simon was the son of John. He had rocklike resources hidden within. Christ reached for the potential!

There are forces silently at work, it would seem, breaking us into fragments. We may give Christ a part of our life but not all of it. We give him a portion of time but reserve the rest for our own use.

Furthermore, we allow ourselves to be split up into classes —clergy and laity, part-time servants or full-time servants. We operate under double standards of ethics and morality. The preacher is supposed to live by one, the laymen by another.

All such is foreign to the teaching of the New Testament and the spirit of Christ's intent. Where does he lay down one requirement for ministers and another for laymen? We are all his disciples. He lays claim to the total man.

Thank God, we are coming into a new day. Laymen are rediscovering ways in which they can use their vast resources and abilities in his kingdom. They are discovering that they can be statesmen, physicians, businessmen, scientists, and at the same time totally committed Christians. Christian living need not be separated from a man's vocation. *Christian living is a man's vocation!*

Dr. Trueblood points out that the first Reformation was made necessary because the professional clergy had usurped powers which did not belong exclusively to them. Among other things they denied "the common man" the right to read and interpret the Bible. He says: "The first Reformation which came to its climax more than three centuries ago produced a great new power by something analogous to a change of gears. As we look back now on that marvelous and rapid development, which did so much to bring democracy to our world, we realize that the crucial step was that of making available the open Bible. . . . The Bible, being a revolutionary document, is naturally an instrument of emancipation. The men and women, who could read the Bible for themselves and thus begin to understand God's will directly, soon developed a radical democracy in church government, and, once they had experience in democratic church government, they were not satisfied without democracy in secular government. Thus democratic practices arose simultaneously on two sides of the Atlantic in the small devout communities, especially those of the nonconformist variety." [2]

The need now is to go a step further and claim this great "lost potential"—the unused resources and talents in all and in every man—for Jesus Christ. "Now, after more than three centuries, we can, if we will, change gears again. Our opportunity for a big step lies in opening the ministry to the ordinary Christian in much the same manner that our ancestors opened Bible reading to the ordinary Christian." [3]

II. THE USE OF OUR LIVES

In our discussion of the new vocation for the Christian we have looked at the urgent world need. Now let us think more specifically about the use to which we can put our lives, and we shall think of it in the context of our larger stewardship.

We are not to think of the stewardship of life in any limited sense. So often we associate it only with the way we use our money or even the money we give to the church. The larger stewardship involves the use of all of life. It has to do with what one is and does as much as it has to do with what one has. This larger stewardship involves a man's inner life and attitudes as well as the outward expression of it. Indeed, there is no area of man's life in all its varied relations that is excluded.

This larger stewardship is not easy. It calls for the utmost of self and service. It is all-inclusive. No corner of one's life in any sphere or relationship is exempt from it. This is what makes it more difficult than the stewardship that is limited to a right administration of material things for Christ and his church. Its requirements are more complex. It is harder to live than it is to give. He who gives liberally may at the same time live unrighteously. Spiritual acts are more difficult than physical. It is easier to kneel than it is to pray. It is easier for one to pay his pledge by mailing a check to the treasurer than it is to go with his family to church to worship God and have fellowship with his people. It is easier to unite with the church than it is to follow Christ as Lord. It is easier to give than to love. It is easier to profess than it is to possess and practice.

1. *Being Our Best Selves*

Modesty becomes a Christian but not false modesty. It is

hypocritical for one to pretend to be something he is not. Jesus condemned men for trying to cover up evil with good. He also had something to say about hiding the good that is in us. He said: "Ye are the light of the world. A city that is set on an hill cannot be hid. Neither do men light a candle, and put it under a bushel, but on a candlestick; and it giveth light unto all that are in the house. Let your light so shine before men, that they may see your good works, and glorify your Father which is in heaven" (Matt. 5:14–16). There is an old saying, "Put your best foot forward." That is not advice to be hypocritical. It is asking us to reveal the best side of our lives.

How many people there are in our churches whose abilities are far, far above the average. They evidence qualities of leadership in the club, the civic organization, their business, but withhold all or most of them from Christ. We need to stop pretending we have nothing to give in his service. Let the light out; uncover it. Let it shine into the dark areas where your light may be the only one.

Your personality is you. It is all of you. It is distinctively you. It is all of the characteristics you have inherited from your ancestors. It is the traits you have acquired or may acquire through study and education. It is the part of you that has come from the environment about you. It is the transformed self that has come as a gift of God's grace. What you are and what you can be is your first and best gift to God. Paul said that the Macedonian Christians "first gave their own selves to the Lord" (2 Cor. 8:5). There is no greater gift.

2. Our Money and Our Lives

The use we make of our money is only a small part of stewardship, but it is a very vital part. Jesus knew the important place money would command in our lives. There is no other single subject to which he gives so much attention. Jesus warned men against its mastery. "No man can serve two masters: for either he will hate the one, and love the other; or else he will hold to the one, and despise the other. Ye cannot serve God and mammon" (Matt. 6:24). He knew it could be the cause of greed and covetousness and strife. "Take heed, and beware of covetousness: for a man's life consisteth not in the abundance of the things which he possesseth" (Luke 12:15). He knew its use or misuse could completely absorb a man's life and determine his eternal destiny. His story of the rich man and his barns reminds us that a man who thinks he possesses everything may in reality possess nothing (Luke 12:16–21). The rich man found that when he faced death his worldly possessions were in reality nothing at all and that his worldly wisdom was really foolishness.

Jesus knew the value of money, and in his parable of the talents (Matt. 6:19–21) urged his disciples to lay up treasures in heaven (Matt. 6:20). He knew that the use of money could reveal the deep devotion of a life to God. Of all the gifts cast into the Temple treasury, the small gift of a humble widow caught his eye and received his commendation (Luke 21:1–4).

We cannot separate money from life. Our money is our life. It represents the labor of our hands and minds. It becomes the channel for our spiritual energy. Nor is the stewardship of our possessions satisfied by setting apart a dedicated portion. The Bible is clear in its teaching concerning our tithes and offerings. We are not likely to be faithful at this point, however, unless we are faithful in the total stewardship of our money. Our stewardship begins not in our giving but in our getting. A man must recognize that he is God's steward in his business—in the way he acquires his wealth. Many a man's generosity in Christ's kingdom has been spoiled because people knew of his unchristian principles in the business of getting wealth. He was not different from his pagan competitors.

Also involved in the stewardship of money is a man's administration of it. A man may piously boast that he is not interested in money and be careless in the way he invests it and spends it—all of it. It was the man in Jesus' story of the talents who put the money to a good and profitable use that won the Master's commendation. Nor will the gift of "dedicated portion"—even a tithe—compensate for the misuse or ill use of the remainder. We are responsible for the way we administer our possessions.

Halford Luccock tells the story of a friend of his who found this statement in a financial journal: "Since the first coin came from the first mint, men have been divided into two groups: Those who work for money and those who put money to work for them." [4] Concerning that statement he makes this observation: "According to this journal of busy finance there is no third group made up of people who make their money work for something higher than themselves. . . . He has completely missed the great host of people, whose total estate varies in quantity from five dollars to five million dollars, who make their money work for human welfare." [5]

That is what money can do. It can be used to extend far beyond the reach of our own lives. As stewards entrusted with a portion of that which belongs to God we can honor him. Every gift we make, every wise use we make of our money can be a recognition of his lordship. It can be used to help other people in bringing to them the blessings of the gospel of Christ. In so doing we are making our money work for something far higher than ourselves.

3. *Using All That We Have*

The larger stewardship involves the use we make of our personality, our money, our time, our all.

Take for instance our talents. Actually, a talent was a measure of money, but it has come to be more inclusive. The principle in Jesus' parable applies to the use of either. We use the word "talent" in its widest sense. Not only as a "particular and uncommon aptitude for some special work or activity," but also for the cultivated ability or power to plan, to direct, and to do. Everyone has resources and powers of some sort and degree which he can harness and bring into action in the service of God. Everyone is a steward of his ability, inherent or cultivated. No person is excused from service for Christ because he does not possess the gifts or aptitudes which someone else has. Our Lord is not asking for talents we do not possess, but he is calling for the faithful stewardship of every talent we have. There is a place and a need in the manifold activities belonging to the progress of the gospel in the world for every kind of ability it is possible for the children of God to possess. No one can truthfully say, "There is nothing I can do."

We mention one other—time. This is a gift that is given to all alike. Like life, it is a gift from God. We cannot create it for ourselves. We can only use it. We cannot do with time as we do with money—lay it away for future use. We must use each moment, each day as it comes to us. Life cannot be crowded into the last few moments. It will be the sum total of all that each day and each year has poured into it. Knowing this, we should make the psalmist's petition our daily prayer. "So teach us to number our days, that we may apply our hearts unto wisdom" (Psalm 90:12).

Moments can be eternally decisive—for ourselves and for others. Said one of our great missionary leaders as he sat at his desk surrounded by the pictures of three of his predecessors who had died in the prime of life, "Young man, what you plan to do, do it today!" Time will not wait on us.

The use of our time will thus be determined by our choice of that which we consider of first importance. On one occasion the enemies of Christ tried to divert him from his purpose. Luke writes: "The same day there came certain of the

Pharisees, saying unto him, Get thee out, and depart hence: for Herod will kill thee. And he said unto them, Go ye, and tell that fox, Behold, I cast out devils, and I do cures to day and to morrow, and the third day I shall be perfected. Nevertheless I must walk to day, and to morrow, and the day following: for it cannot be that a prophet perish out of Jerusalem" (Luke 13:31–33). There was a goal to be reached; there was work to be done; he would use the time at hand to accomplish that purpose. It was that use of time that crowded eternity into the brief span of his years. He used all his life—his time, his remarkable capacities, his influence for the glory of the Father, He lived with all he had under a sense of divine mission. That is the way God meant each life, large or small, to be lived. That is the Christian's vocation.

III. THAT MAN MAY KNOW

What is the Christian's first and highest business? What is the purpose of this new vocation to which he has been called —this total dedication of his life to Christ? What is the mission of the church—Christians working together in and through this fellowship?

The answer is found in the mission of Christ himself. What did God send him to do? What was the mission he committed to his followers, his church—then and now?

"The Son of man is come to seek and to save that which was lost" (Luke 19:10). Thus Jesus defined his mission. That mission he entrusted to his disciples, his church, every one who would follow him. "Come ye after me, and I will make you to become fishers of men" (Mark 1:17). "As my Father hath sent me, even so send I you" (John 20:21). In his final words to his disciples Luke catches both the content of the message and the responsibility for its delivery. "Thus it is written, and thus it behoved Christ to suffer, and to rise from the dead the third day: and that repentance and remission of sins should be preached in his name among all nations, be-

ginning at Jerusalem. And ye are witnesses of these things" (Luke 24:46–48).

This, then is the supreme purpose of the individual Christian and of the church. We must of necessity do many things. We come together for worship and fellowship. We should stand as the moral conscience against the corruption in the world. We should speak and act for justice, peace, equality. We should be guided by the motive of service. We should teach "all things" that he left for us.

All of this is good. All of it can be in keeping with the correct purpose. But it is all dedicated to this one end: declaring the good news to all people that Jesus Christ is the Saviour and Lord for all who will believe in and surrender to him.

As another puts it: "The Christian thrust in the world includes proclamation (Kerygma), service (diakonia), fellowship (koinonia), teaching (didache). To neglect any of these imperatives is to jeopardize all. Yet the church exists in the world always as a divinely forged beachhead sheltering wicked men otherwise exposed to the wrath of a holy God. Unless she burns with the realization of a world in spiritual revolt and doomed to judgment, having no guarantee of survival, let alone of the good life and eternal bliss, apart from a saving relationship to Jesus Christ, the church easily misconceives and miscarries her mission." [6]

1. The World Challenge

That little handful of first-century Christians took Jesus' commission seriously. The odds of the pagan world of Rome were against them. Yet, so effective was their strategy, so fervent was their passion, so faithful was their witness that by the middle of the fourth century the direction of the whole Roman Empire had been so changed that the character (or nature) of European life and Western civilization would thereafter be radically changed.

Unfortunately that fervor and faithfulness to our chief

task has not continued. There have been great surges forward in world evangelism across the centuries. The great Christian leader and statesmen, John R. Mott, challenged the World Missions Conference in Edinburgh in 1910 with the slogan, "The World for Christ in this generation." Billy Graham, in our time, has preached to more people around the world than any preacher since Christianity was launched. Yet, the tide runs against us. We are not winning the world for Christ; we are losing it!

Even if we could reach everyone in this generation the burst of population outruns us. As someone has reminded us, "We are always just one generation from becoming pagan."

We are failing to keep abreast of the "population explosion" which now predicts a world population by 1980 of 4,280,000,000 people! And the latest total is already in need of revising upward. Moreover, there are mighty forces at work to win the world to their way of life.

Godless communism presses forward on many fronts laying claim to world conquest domination. Its increase from a small beginning forty odd years ago to its present control over half the world's population staggers man's wildest imagination. In addition to that, "Pagan religions are on the march. Mohammedanism in fact now claims to have in Africa alone more missionaries than Protestantism has in all the world. Buddhists are expanding and adapting their program, setting Buddhist doctrines to Christian hymnody (for example, 'Buddha loves me, this I know'). By systematic revision the Hindu sacred writings are being made intelligible to the masses. Already building bigger shrines, Shintoism in the next decade hopes to restore emperor worship to Japan. Roman Catholicism with all its aberrations is maneuvering again to speak for a united Christendom. The cults of Jehovah's Witnesses and Mormonism are surging ahead with new life." [7]

All this gives unparalleled urgency to the Christian witness if we are even to hold our own in this world, much less take it for Christ.

2. *Every Christian's Job*

If we are to turn the tide in world evangelization it must become every Christian's personal responsibility. We are grateful for one man who can command the attention of crowds numbering into the hundreds of thousands around the world with the simple proclamation of the gospel of Christ. God alone can measure the good he will do, the numbers he will lead to an acceptance of the Saviour.

We are indebted beyond our ability to express to that noble few who carry the banner for our foreign mission program. But when there are only a few Christian workers numbered among thousands and even millions, they will not get the job done!

The strategy of Jesus and the New Testament was that every follower would become a witness. There was no distinction between laity and clergy. Those who found Christ as Saviour were moved by an inner impulse, a deep and compassionate concern to share the good news with others. A woman of sordid character found the water of life at his hands and went back among those with whom she had sinned to say: "Come, see a man, which told me all things that ever I did: is not this the Christ?" (John 4:29).

Perhaps herein lies the fault—we cannot share what we have not experienced. We cannot tell what we do not know. We cannot demonstrate what we do not have—life in Christ.

Vital Christian witness is born of firsthand experience—not hearsay. If one has met Christ and in him found forgiveness for his own sins, the release of new power that came from his living Spirit, a new purpose for living, then he has something to tell to which other men may well listen. This was the strategy of those who followed Christ. "For I delivered to you as of first importance what I also received, that

Christ died for our sins in accordance with the scriptures, that he was buried, that he was raised on the third day in accordance with the scriptures" (1 Cor. 15:3–4, RSV). That was Paul's message. It is ours.

We must never forget—even in our age of the mass mind, the organization man—that vital evangelism must be kept "person to person." Someone speaking of a prominent preacher of another generation said, "When I went into his study, his great figure seemed to fill the room and overpower me. I had the feeling that he loved the whole world so dearly that he did not love anyone especially!" That was not God's way. He did love the whole world dearly but he loved every man especially. He expressed that love ultimately and forever in the person, Jesus Christ. When Christ came he wore our garments, touched our lives at all their sore, earthy spots, died at last on a cross not only for all men but also for each man—even a lonely thief who died on a cross next to his.

The world waits on each man who names Christ's name to assume the responsibility for sharing his life with every man he meets or can find.

3. *Unto the Uttermost*

Evangelism begins with the individual; it knows no geographical boundaries. "Ye shall be witnesses unto me both in Jerusalem, and in all Judaea, and in Samaria, and unto the uttermost part of the earth" (Acts 1:8).

The age of isolation—never compatible with the Christian concept—has passed from our world. We are involved in mankind. We can no longer ignore what happens in Cuba, Tibet, or the Congo. We are all swept along on the same current.

As followers of the universal Christ we are involved in the evangelization of the world. In the past, and perhaps for organizational purposes in the future, we must divide responsibility—the work of the local church, associational missions, state missions, home missions, foreign missions. But the new concept for the new day is not to see missions departmentalized but to see the mission of the church as one. That mission is not the function of some organization in the church or a special group of people. It is the whole church in action. It is the body of Christ expressing Christ's concern for the whole world. This mission is the purpose for the very existence of the church. The church was called into being to win the whole world to Christ. When she repudiates that mission she ceases to be the church.

When we speak of the "mission of the church" we mean everything that the church is sent into the world to do—preach the gospel, heal the sick, care for the poor, teach the children, improve international and interracial relations, attack injustice—all of this and more can rightly be included in the phrase "the mission of the church." But all of this is for the purpose of witnessing to Jesus Christ.

Says Donald Miller: "The mission of the church, therefore, is to extend to men of 'every tribe and tongue and people and nation' the glad news of Jesus' redemptive love for them. The charter of the church was given by Jesus: 'You shall be my *witnesses* in Jerusalem and in all Judea and Samaria and to the end of the earth' (Acts 1:8). Should the new Israel fail in this, she would but repeat the tragedy of the old Israel. And the fate of the old Israel likewise would be hers. The church can only be the church as she realizes that her very life is mission." [8]

In the fulfilment of that mission the church must seek to carry its message to the uttermost part of the earth with all possible haste. In so doing it must be remembered that Christ is not for the whole world simply geographically but for the whole man. Evangelism must not be thought of only in terms of "soul saving" but of "life saving" also. There must be no "lost provinces" unclaimed by Christ. We must seek to win the whole world but also the whole man—physically, mentally, emotionally, socially.

Only when we get this concept of the gospel of Jesus Christ for all men and for the whole man can we hope to offer him our lives dedicated to a new vocation—fulfilling the purpose of God in Christ for time and eternity.

FOR FURTHER STUDY AND DISCUSSION

1. Discuss some of the present world conditions that give such urgency for world evangelization.
2. We recommend Elton Trueblood's *Your Other Vocation* as an excellent book for additional study and discussion of this subject.
3. Explore what your church may do to discover the "lost provinces" and "lost potential" within your membership.
4. Use the stewardship parables of Jesus as a basis for discussion of the larger stewardship of life.
5. Discuss ways in which we can use more of our people in winning the world for Christ.

CHAPTER 8 OUTLINE

I. THE WORLD THAT CAN BE SHAKEN

    1. The Pending World Disaster

    2. Social Insecurity

    3. The Mirage of Plenty

    4. The Last Line of Defense

II. WHEN THE TROUBLE GETS INSIDE

    1. The Crisis of Frustration

    2. The Crisis of Anxiety

    3. The Crisis of Tragedy

    4. The Crises of Doubt

III. THE THINGS THAT REMAIN

    1. The Unseen Is Real

    2. The Certainty of God

    3. Our Eternal Contemporary

    4. The Cross o'er the Wrecks of Time

IV. STRENGTH FOR THE INNER CITADEL

    1. Finding Christ's Kind of Peace

    2. Finding Christ's Kind of Power

    3. Beyond the Last Horizon

8

In a Troubled World—
a New Security

"IN THE WORLD you have tribulation; but be of good cheer, I have overcome the world" (John 16:33, RSV). With these words Jesus set the stage for the Christian's conquest. He would secure followers under no false pretenses. The going would be hard; the cost would be high. No quarter would be asked. "Warning," he said, "there is danger ahead!"

The clouds of the impending storm were already dark on the horizon. Soon it would break and take him to the cross. He would not ask that his disciples be exempt from suffering —then or ever. That was what they must expect in their world. It is what we can expect in ours.

Yet, neither he, nor they, nor we, were to be carried to defeat. "Courage," he assured, "I have conquered the world!" Those words have been called "the most gallant words in literature." Think of it. He was about to be betrayed, forsaken, crucified by the cruel forces of evil. In the face of all that he had the daring faith to say: "Be of good cheer; the victory will be mine and yours." In a troubled world that is the Christian's kind of security.

I. THE WORLD THAT CAN BE SHAKEN

In this kind of a world there is no assurance that the things we thought would remain will remain. The author of the letter to the Hebrew Christians makes this observation concerning his world. "'Yet once more I will shake not only the earth but also the heaven.' This phrase, 'Yet once more,' indicates the removal of *what is shaken*." (Hebrews 12:26–27,

RSV). That is to say, there are some things that we may well expect to succumb to the processes of destruction.

Bear in mind that the author of Hebrews was living in a world dominated by Rome, the Eternal City. This way of life seemed destined to last forever. Those of the Jewish faith who had turned Christian knew better. The institutions and way of life which they had cherished in other days were gone. The Temple was destroyed, the altar desecrated, the sacrifices discontinued, the priesthood vanquished. Their world had been shaken. By the end of the fourth century Rome also would know that. That which seems so stable, so changeless today can be suddenly shaken to pieces.

1. *The Pending World Disaster*

Since that fateful summer day in 1945 when the first atomic bomb burst over Hiroshima, Japan, we know how sudden and complete that destruction can be.

Today that force has been multiplied a thousandfold. There is no need to recite figures—even if they were available. In a year's time or a month's they would be out of date. In the face of this growing, frightening power, the United State's representative to the United Nations has on several occasions invited Russia to join us in halting the making of nuclear weapons "for the sake of all mankind."

Well might the world powers heed that plea, for they hold now in their hands the potential power to destroy not only Western civilization but all mankind.

That which we thought secure can be taken from us. And even barring the holocaust of a nuclear war, the world revolution is slowly changing many of the things we thought would last. Ideas, habits, institutions, ethical standards—once apparently solid and durable—now seem to many "frail as frost landscapes on a windowpane." Nuclear power makes everything on earth seem perishable.

2. Social Insecurity

There are forces at work much closer home that affect the society of which we are a part.

We are a people on the move—a nomadic people in a non-nomadic society. First it was a movement from the rural areas to the great urban centers. Now it is the movement from center to circumference within the city. We are fast becoming a suburban society. Or, it is the movement from city to city. We are a transient society. What does all of this mean? It means that there are millions of our people who never live in any one place long enough to put down roots and grow. They do not know the security of established community life.

There are definite stabilizing effects that come from becoming a part of a community. People on the move often find it difficult to make contact with "the church of their parents." Consequently they lose interest and deny their children the privilege of Christian worship and education which their parents afforded them.

The public school can be another stabilizing force. How much has it meant to some of us who lived in one community all our lives. The teachers who taught and influenced us, and the friends we made have been hands of strength holding us through the years. On the other hand, we can never measure the disastrous consequences that may come to a child's sense of security by removing him from one school to another every few years, uprooting him from a friendly and familiar environment.

The same is true of the entire community. We sometimes do not know our neighbors; often they do not know us. We appear to feel no sense of responsibility or concern for one another. I once went to a certain street in my city where there had been a death in the family. Not having the exact address,

I inquired of one of the neighbors. They knew nothing of a death in that community. When I finally found the right house, I discovered it was just next door to the unknowing neighbor. This is a small world, indeed, but often two houses side by side can be worlds apart!

When we are on the move we do not feel a part of society. We accept little or no responsibility for its welfare. We do not know the strength that can come by being a part of the life of the church, the school, the neighborhood. We are victims of social insecurity. To whom can we turn in the hour of need?

3. *The Mirage of Plenty*

In an age of plenty, material values have predominated over all others. The rising cost of living has forced us to keep everlastingly at it just to keep ahead. "Keeping up with the Joneses" has often imposed upon us a standard that we are not reasonably able to maintain. The dedication of Russia to the "god of materialistic progress" would force us to try to keep up with them or outstrip them at the sacrifice of all other values. Materialism has become the goal of success, the measure of all progress.

"Time magazine has indicted the generation for its 'cautious' desire to be 'well fixed.' In a study of two thousand young people eighteen to twenty-nine years of age conducted by the Y.M.C.A. it was found that 76 per cent of those who discussed future aspirations were seeking primarily respectability and security: security in terms of material goods, security in terms of one's own little family circle, security in terms of acceptance and respect in one's own circle of acquaintance. One answer, possibly typical of the average, came from a young man: 'The most important thing in life is to be successful. . . . I'd like to be happy and have plenty of money. I'd like to be married and have a nice home, kids and a good reputation in the community.' " [1]

It is not surprising, therefore, that for millions of people, success means material success, and security means financial security. We look to hospitalization to care for us when we are born and when we are sick. We are counting on "Social Security" to provide for us at retirement. We have "insurance" that will bury us when we die. From the cradle to the grave material provision has been made to care for us.

The tragedy is that all this is not security. No one would underestimate the value of wise planning for financial security in time of emergency, but we should all know that it is a mirage in a desert of want if that is all we have.

With what force Jesus drove this truth home in his story of the rich man building bigger barns to care for his great harvest. For this man was saying exactly what we so often say or feel: "And he said, 'I will do this: I will pull down my barns, and build larger ones; and there I will store all my grain and my goods. And I will say to my soul, Soul, you have ample goods laid up for many years; take your ease, eat, drink, be merry'" (Luke 12:18–19, RSV). He had all that he would need—now or ever—or so he thought. Then it was that God confronted him with his poverty—the poverty of his soul. He had no spiritual security. God said to him, "'Fool! This night your soul is required of you; and the things you have prepared, whose will they be?' So is he who lays up treasure for himself, and is not rich toward God" (Luke 12:20–21, RSV).

What the rich man considered everything turned out to be nothing. One's life is made secure not by things, but by the triumph over things. In our mad quest for material security we shall be weighed and found wanting.

4. *The Last Line of Defense*

One of the gravest threats to our security, whether it be social, national, or personal, is the threat to the slowly disintegrating American family life.

It is in the home that a man and a woman have found such courage and strength from each other that the two have been more than two. It is in the home that the child has found its best environment and resources for physical, mental, and spiritual challenge and growth. There he first learns what it means to be wanted and loved and needed. It is in the home that society has found its greatest hope for the future, its bulwark against the enemies of society. It is to the home that we must turn to find leadership and character adequate for our world.

When something happens to the home life as it is happening in our nation today a vital blow is being struck at the very heart of our whole society. The alarming increase in infidelity and divorce, the rising tide of juvenile crime, the breakdown of moral responsibility in the home is like an earthquake—it is shaking our society to pieces, and no one can escape the consequences.

II. When the Trouble Gets Inside

In the outside world we can expect trouble. The trouble really begins, however, when it gets on the inside of us. As one mother put it when she received word of the death of her last son right at the close of the war, with shouts of triumph all around that their way of life had been made secure in the world: "But my world is such a little world." World conditions for her seemed of little consequence. Tragedy had penetrated her own inner world.

The external events that swirl about us are impartial. In one way or another they come to all of us alike—war, tragedies of nature, economic reverses, sickness, death. Jesus said: "He maketh his sun to rise on the evil and on the good, and sendeth rain on the just and on the unjust" (Matt. 5:45). God does not play favorites. What makes the difference? It depends upon the inwardness of life. If the trouble gets on the inside, like the sea water breaking through the dykes, our whole inner world is washed by the brackish, deadening effect of our moods. Here we can deal with only a few of them.

1. *The Crisis of Frustration*

After World War I the rising generation was called "the lost generation." In our time a new mood prevails. This is "the beat generation." Why is it so called? Many have summed it up as "a lost sense of purpose." They seem to be unable to find any worthwhile reason for living.

What has happened that has brought about such a mood? Perhaps it is because the victories that have been won have all come to nothing—they turned to ashes in our hands. We fought and won two terrible wars but to what purpose? We fought a limited war in Korea but there was never a clear-cut triumph. Such has been the struggle in our time—always a war or a "war of nerves" or a "cold war" but never any satisfying achievement, never any arriving.

Often we have achieved goals to find them unsatisfying. We become "successful"; we have what it takes to satisfy the basic hunger for food and drink, sex and play, but they don't really satisfy. There is still a deep, gnawing hunger.

So we have dreamed dreams and seen visions and followed the rainbows for the pots of gold, and we have never found the fulfilment, or finding, we have been disappointed. The mood of frustration swept over our souls. "What's the use?" we have cried. Life is suffering from frustration and defeat.

2. *The Crisis of Anxiety*

Pick up almost any book today that has to do with our personal crises, and you will find one of the major problems to be anxiety. No doubt historians of the future will call our time the age of anxiety.

With that analysis few of us would argue. "W. H. Auden has called ours the 'Age of Anxiety.' Albert Camus calls this the 'century of fear.' Anxiety is the most common affliction of our age. We see it on every hand—people afraid of the past, fearful of the future, people whose lives have broken down under the strain of unrelieved anxiety. Our hospitals are crowded with patients suffering from anxiety neuroses. Other millions live out their lives in the shadows of fear." [2]

Anxiety in our time is not without reason. Many factors contribute to it. We are all but lost in an awful maze of uncertainty. World events are rushing toward an unpredictable climax. The character of many of those in places of power is such that we cannot trust them. Add to that our own personal uncertainties—our job, our children, our health.

"It is ironic," writes one, "that we feel most insecure at a time when we are trying most desperately to provide 'social security' for everybody. On the face of it, we ought to feel secure. We have been promised security in old age, security in unemployment, security in illness, but with all the promises we feel insecure. Paradoxically, we feel the insecurity of security. We have an uneasy suspicion that the promised security itself is insecure." [3]

Once we open the gates of our inner life to those anxieties—either actual or imaginary—a real crisis develops in our own lives. At best our strength and energy are sapped by fruitless worry. Many people go to their homes physically and mentally exhausted at the end of the day, not because they are overworked but because they have carried too heavy a load of anxieties. One hundred per cent of the fatigue of sedentary workers in good health is due to emotional factors. The emotions in question are listed as: worry, frustration, jealousy, anger, envy, and a wide variety of fears.

If this is allowed to go unchecked, if we find no cure for our anxieties, we can even be swept from our moorings and join that ever-growing number of mentally distraught people who have literally "worried themselves sick."

3. *The Crisis of Tragedy*

Our concern that something may happen to us is not altogether imaginary. Things do happen to us. They are of such nature as to change the course of a whole life. They take many forms. A tornado strikes, and a family's possessions are suddenly swept away. A husband goes to the hospital for a checkup. He is found to be the victim of cancer; he can never be well. A young woman collapses on the way home from work. She has polio of the worst kind. The rest of her life she will be an invalid. Perhaps it is a moral tragedy involving a friend, a member of one's own family. We live under the shadow that is worse than some physical infirmity.

Few, if any of us, escape. Sooner or later, it seems, sickness, sorrow, suffering will get around to most of us. One day we shall open the book of life and find the word "tragedy" penned next to our name.

Although we cannot escape the tragic event that may come to us, the real tragedy occurs when the mood created by it gets on the inside of us. We may try to imagine that it does not exist and indulge in the mood of "escapism." We may follow the advice of Job's wife and curse God that he made us and this sorry scheme of things. We may open our heart to the spirit of resentment, blaming others for our misfortunes. We may stoically grit our teeth and harden our feelings, bear our burdens, endure our hardships—alone.

Here again the same events happen to all of us. The same wind blows over a stagnant pool of water that blows over a rose garden. In one instance it bears a foul odor; in the other, a sweet fragrance. The same rain falls upon molten iron that falls upon fertile soil. The first it makes hard and brittle, the other it makes fruitful. The difference is in the inwardness of life. What happens to trouble us and to us generally depends upon the way we meet it within the citadel of our own soul.

4. *The Crisis of Doubt*

In almost any form of tragedy—sickness, suffering, sorrow —the real crisis develops when the problem begins to impinge upon us personally. As long as we discuss it as a world problem or an academic problem we can look at it quite objectively. Then it happens to us. It tears at our own inner being. Says Carl Michalson, "A man can stand almost anything if he knows it will not last forever, and technology has mercifully abridged the time span of suffering. But what of the suffering that still remains when technologies have reached their limit: the malignancies whose outcome is sure and swift, the disabilities which are as irrevocable as loss of limb, and the curtaining off of sensory channels to a total life? Where in all the technological meanings is there an answer to the cruelest suffering of all, the suffering inherent in the cry, 'Why did this happen to me?' " [4]

Yet, that question we will ask, and it is no sin to ask it. To try to find meaning in that experience, to try to see what we have done to deserve it, to try to understand how such things can happen in the world of "a God of love" has been the searching quest of the greatest of men. It came even to our Lord in his hour of suffering: "My God, my God, why hast thou forsaken me?" (Matt. 27:46).

No, doubt is not disgrace. Doubt is not cynicism. Cynicism is bitterness; it is unbelief. It sees no good in anything. Life has lost its meaning. Doubt is the soul in search of meaning. Doubt is faith in search of a deeper dimension. Cynicism turns its back on God. Doubt tries to look through the clouds to see the face of God more clearly. Paul saw that face and found that purpose when he said: "We know that in everything God works for good with those who love him, who are called according to his purpose" (Rom. 8:28, RSV).

As long as we keep our faces toward him we will find our

way out and through. It is only when doubt turns to cynicism that we shall lose our way.

III. The Things That Remain

In the midst of his world that could be shaken the writer to the Hebrew Christians was aware of those things that would remain—"a kingdom that cannot be shaken" (Heb. 12:28, RSV). In another place he says, "We have this as a sure and steadfast anchor of the soul" (Heb. 6:19, RSV).

In such a time as his he needed that. When so many things he had cherished and counted on were being swept aside like straws in the wind he needed something that was steadfast and abiding. In our kind of a world we need that. This generation has had one certainty after another taken away. The rug has been pulled from under its feet; it has no fixtures to stand on.

Often it is necessary for that which can be shaken to be taken away so that we may turn to that which cannot be shaken. To some of those eternal verities we now give our attention.

1. *The Unseen Is Real*

Too often have we put our confidence in things that we can handle and measure and see. These alone, we have been led to believe, have ultimate reality. Now, if we are wise, we will see that this is not so. Financial security can be taken from us. Political kingdoms change and die. Man-made institutions are transient. We need faith to see the reality of the unseen. As a blind friend of mine used to say: "People say 'seeing is believing,' but I say, 'believing is seeing.'" By his very blindness he came to a deeper sense of reality. He believed that faith itself would enable him to lay hold upon it.

This has ever been the hidden force back of those who

have sought for "a city, not made with hands," a city that has foundations beyond man's unstable existence. As the writer of Hebrews says: "Now faith is the assurance of things hoped for, the conviction of things not seen" (Heb. 11:1, RSV). Or, as Phillips translates it: "Now faith means putting our full confidence in the things we hope for; it means being certain of things we cannot see" (Heb. 11:1, Phillips).

Here within man is the faculty that binds his soul to a fixed reality—faith, hope, love, and God himself. This is not wishful thinking. It is not the wild dream of an idealist. Men have ventured forth believing that God could be trusted and that his universe would not lie. The record of their incredible achievements stands for all to read. They were ever searching for a deeper reality, believing that God would validate their faith. He did not disappoint them. He will not disappoint us. For "We look not at the things which are seen, but at the things which are not seen: for the things which are seen are temporal; but the things which are not seen are eternal" (2 Cor. 4:18).

2. *The Certainty of God*

Faith in the unseen does not go far enough. It must lead us to Ultimate Reality—to the One we can trust. It is because of him that the invisible qualities of love and faith and hope have meaning. So it is God who gives abiding quality and meaning to all else. As Arthur Hugh Clough writes:

> It fortifies my soul to know
> That, though I perish, Truth is so:
> That, howsoe'er I stray and range,
> Whate'er I do, Thou dost not change.
> I steadier step when I recall
> That, if I slip thou dost not fall.[5]

Nothing less than this will satisfy the soul's quest for security—nothing less than God himself. So says the author of Hebrews: . . . "we who are refugees from this dying world might have a source of strength, and might grasp the hope that he holds out to us. This hope we hold as the utterly reliable anchor for our souls, fixed in the very certainty of God himself" (Heb. 6:19–20, Phillips).

When we lay hold upon the certainty of God then we no longer depend upon the things we have made or upon our own strength. We are "kept by the power of God through faith" (1 Peter 1:5). We are held not by our faith alone but by the certainty of God.

3. *Our Eternal Contemporary*

God is spirit; he is eternal; he is omnipotent. He is beyond our knowing, yet, he is knowable. He is above and before and beyond time. Yet, he is in time. With each new flash of revelation across the centuries man saw some facet of his nature and gave him another name.

God's revelation of himself reached its climax in Jesus Christ. He carried into time the full accent of eternity. He vocalized God. To use John's great term, he was the Word. Elsewhere of course, in nature, in the voice of history, in our own intuitions, there are broken syllables, but Jesus is the full-spoken Word.

Christ is our eternal contemporary. He reaches back as far as God. He reaches ahead as long as time will last—and beyond. He is "the same yesterday, and to day, and for ever" (Heb. 13:8). He is both timeless and timely. He meets our needs today. He is abreast and ever ahead of our times. George Matheson in his *Studies of the Portrait of Christ* writes: "In the culture of the past, Thou, Christ, art the only modern. No one else felt the need and sympathy of man for man. . . . Thou hast broken the barriers of caste! Thou hast reached the last motive of charity, which is the right of the hungry for bread. Thou hast outrun our philanthropy. Thou hast anticipated our benevolence. Thou hast modeled our infirmaries and orphanages. Thou hast sketched our asylums.

Thou hast devised our homes of refuge. . . . Thou hast asserted the sacredness of infant life. Thou hast given a hand to the climbing steps of woman. At the end of all our progress we meet Thee." [6]

In Christ we have the man of the hour—dealing with each moment as if it were eternity—as indeed it is. He is also the man of the centuries—belonging to all men of every age and every race and giving eternal significance to each moment. For nineteen centuries he has haunted the thinking and conscience of mankind—Judge and Saviour, Servant and King. He is our eternal contemporary. He will abide ever the same.

4. The Cross o'er the Wrecks of Time

Why has the cross endured as the symbol of our faith? Why not a star or a palm branch or a yoke? All of them—and many other symbols—were associated with Christ. Is it not because the cross has to do with that which is eternal—in God and in man?

Joseph Fort Newton gives us this story that points toward the deeper meaning. "Florence Converse has a story, 'Crux Ave, Spes Unica,' in which Mr. Budget, blueprint in hand, proposes to take down an old Cross as a thing out of date and unsightly. He intends to erect in its place a short-wave radio station, to broadcast a modern religion with no Cross in it. The wrecking crew tries, with ropes, ladders and tools, to pull the old Cross down—warning a poor 'lunatic,' the only sane man on the scene, not to let it fall on him. Having failed to pull it down, they try to dig it up, but that fails too. The 'lunatic' tells them why: 'They can't pull it over, they can't dig it up. It's from the beginning. It's the core of creation.'" [7]

So it is. The cross was in the heart and mind of God. It is woven into the very fabric of the universe. It cast its dim shadow across Eden. Its anguish is in Abraham's uplifted arm. Its heartbreak is in Hosea's story of pathos and love. It is in every struggle of our Saviour from the wilderness to Gethsemane. Like the crimson strand that is found in the ropes of the British Navy it is woven into the very fabric of God's purpose.

The cross is a human necessity. Sin came to destroy everything good and beautiful that God had designed. It would not be satisfied until it had taken God's best gift and nailed him to the cross. Whatever else the cross may mean it stands over the wrecks of human lives saying: "This is what the power of sin can do."

The cross is also a divine necessity. God's love for men meant that he must find a way of redemption. The way he chose—and it was before the foundation of the world—was the cross. And the cross is but the symbol of God's suffering love. The struggle between man's sin and God's love is an ageless struggle, but it culminated in the white heat of combat on Calvary. There God's best engaged sin's worst and conquered. The cross shall ever stand against man's blackened sky and over the wrecks he has made of his world and himself to remind us that there is no cheap or easy solution to the problem of sin. It cost God the life of his Son.

As long, then, as man needs a Saviour and as long as God's love goes out to meet that need the cross remains man's last, best hope in a shaken world.

> In the cross of Christ I glory,
> Tow'ring o'er the wrecks of time,
> All the light of sacred story
> Gathers round its head sublime.

IV. STRENGTH FOR THE INNER CITADEL

Christ warned us that our lives were destined to be lived out in a troubled world. If we expect to find strength and security from our environment we are doomed to disappointment. We need to discover a source of inner security—something that the world cannot give us or take from us.

In our troubled world that is our ultimate need. We are so constantly up against unsolved and insurmountable problems that we are spiritually exhausted. The demands of life are so great that our inner sources of strength are depleted. Those who deal with the human problems—the minister, the psychiatrist, the counselor—are recognizing more and more the poverty of man's inner life: He does not build up emotional and spiritual reserves adequate for his day.

We need to give attention to the fortifying of the inner citadel of life. That was the secret of Christ's serenity in a troubled world. It can be ours.

1. Finding Christ's Kind of Peace

Christ's kind of peace! What thrilling words those are for a strife-torn world and for people who are searching everywhere for peace of mind.

The thing that makes these words meaningful is that they were spoken by one who knew much trouble. Almost all his active life was lived under bitter opposition and struggle. When he spoke those memorable words, "Peace I leave with you, my peace I give unto you" (John 14:27), he was walking into the shadow of Gethsemane and the cross. For him, it would seem, there was everything but peace. Yet there was within the citadel of his soul a calmness that has continued to amaze and bless those who have come to know him. It is his legacy to a troubled and uneasy world.

What kind of peace was it that made it so utterly different from the peace the world gives? It is certainly not a peace that is dependent upon outward circumstances. It is not the peace of a sheltered pool, unrippled and motionless; that is stagnation. It is not a peace that knows no trouble or has no concern for those who do. It is not a kind of surface peace—

a pretense that cries, "Peace, peace" when life within is torn by turmoil.

Christ's kind of peace is that which stands sentinel at the gateway of the soul, that marches into our hearts and minds like a garrison defending the inner citadel of life. It is not the kind of peace that the world knows or can give. It is a gift from God. It can belong to that life whose trust is in him and whose life is committed to the doing of his will. It is a peace with God that man knows in his heart when all about him is struggle and confusion.

2. *Finding Christ's Kind of Power*

Our feeling of insecurity often comes from our sense of inadequacy. We take the measure of our world—or today's problem, for that matter—and become frightened and apprehensive because we are no match for it.

What kind of power did Christ have to match the world of his day and ours? How did he purpose to conquer a world that was dominated by a vastly superior force like Rome? Who but a fool would dare say, "Be of good cheer; I have overcome the world" (John 16:33)? Yet, he did dare make that affirmation. And the most incredible thing is that his power was neither in the vast power at his disposal in the physical universe nor in some fearful and shattering act of judgment. Rather, it was in what took place [or occurred] on Calvary. "And I, if I be lifted up from the earth, will draw all men unto me" (John 12:32). It was the power of love—God's kind of love over all the forces of this world. Neither hate, nor selfishness, nor even death could conquer him. Through his atoning death and resurrection he released a power that nothing could stop.

That was Christ's power—a power that could take the worst sin in the world and command and defeat it, or turn it to serve his purpose. The forces of evil handed him a cross, but when he had finished with it it had become the world's greatest symbol of victory—for his time and ours and forever.

With this power Christ's few disciples went forth to conquer the world. It was with this power that Paul stormed the citadel of Rome's strength. His battle cry was: "I am not ashamed of the gospel of Christ: for it is the power of God unto salvation to every one that believeth" (Rom. 1:16).

Christ never sought security in some impregnable fortress. He never recommended safety first. Security for the Christian has ever been on the battle line. The only safe movement for those who follow Christ is forward. He never asked us to find little jobs equal to our strength. He promised us power equal to world-shaking conquest. Not in some underground shelter will we find security in the nuclear age but in moving ahead for him and with him—in tension and in struggle—to win a world! Then and only then does he promise—"Lo, I am with you" (Matt. 28:20).

This is Christ's gift to us in our time. It is the source of our confidence in a world where the odds are constantly against us. If Christ be for us that's all that matters. If the citadel is garrisoned with his strength nothing can ultimately defeat us.

3. *Beyond the Last Horizon*

What about death? "If a man die," Job asked, "shall he live again?" There is no "if" here. Sooner or later death will come to all. So goes the old legend of a merchant in Baghdad. One day he sent his servant to the market. Before very long the servant came back white and trembling, and in great agitation said to his master, "Down in the market place I was jostled by a woman in the crowd, and when I turned around I saw it was Death that jostled me. She looked at me and made a threatening gesture. Oh, Master, lend me your horse, for I must hasten away to avoid my fate. I will ride to Samarra and there I will hide and Death will not find me."

The merchant lent him his horse and the servant galloped away in great haste. Later the merchant went down to the market place and saw Death standing in the crowd. He went over to her and asked, "Why did you frighten my servant this morning? Why did you make a threatening gesture?"

"That was not a threatening gesture," Death said. "It was only a start of surprise. I was astonished to see him in Baghdad, for I have an appointment with him tonight in Samarra."

So death has an appointment with all of us. Even if the inner citadel can hold out against all that can happen to us here on earth, what assurance do we have of victory over death?

There is, of course, man's "invincible surmise" that he is immortal. Job in his troubled life believed that death was not the final act. "For I know that my redeemer liveth, and that he shall stand at the latter day upon the earth (Job 19:25). The Greek philosopher, Socrates, discussed the possibility of immortality often with his pupils. Even the infidel has not always been able to escape it. Confronted with the death of his brother, Robert Ingersoll said, "What lies beyond? From the voiceless lips of the unreplying dead there comes no word; but in the night of death hope sees a star, and listening love can hear the rustle of a wing." In his immortal poem Tennyson wrote:

> Thou madest man, he knows not why,
> He thinks he was not made to die.

In answer to this ageless hope comes the clear and triumphant word of Christ. "I am the resurrection, and the life: he that believeth in me, though he were dead, yet shall he live: And whosoever liveth and believeth in me shall never die" (John 11:25–26).

This was no mere "surmise" on immortality. It rested upon the solid foundation of what had happened on that early Sunday morning in the garden long ago. "Why seek ye the living among the dead? He is not here, but is risen" (Luke 24:5–6).

This his followers saw for themselves. This became their

transforming experience. This was their witness to a dead and dying world. "I delivered unto you first of all that which I also received, how that Christ died for our sins according to the scriptures; and that he was buried, and that he rose again the third day according to the scriptures" (1 Cor. 15:3–4). It was the message for those dead in trespasses and sins. It was their one reliable hope for a new life in Christ. And it was more; it was the basis for their hope that life would go beyond what we call death to an ultimate and glorious fulfilment. "His resurrection was the triumph of the life that was in him over all the powers of darkness and death which seemed, and still seem, to rule in the outward world. *Not death and fear, but life and love, are the ultimates.*" [8]

The security of the new life in Christ rests neither upon man's surmise nor his hope but upon the strength of God's eternal love and purpose. In that ultimate purpose extended to us in the death and resurrection of our Lord Jesus Christ is our security—now and forever. "For I am persuaded, that neither death, nor life, nor angels, nor principalities, nor powers, nor things present, nor things to come, nor height, nor depth, nor any other creature, shall be able to separate us from the love of God, which is in Christ Jesus our Lord" (Rom. 8:38–39).

And so we pass from the inner citadel in which Christ dwells into "an house not made with hands, eternal in the heavens" (2 Cor. 5:1).

That is the word to us and it is the word of God, and we can trust him beyond all else no matter what happens. "I know," says Paul, "whom I have believed, and am persuaded that he is able to keep that which I have committed unto him against that day" (2 Tim. 1:12).

That is the new life that can be ours in Christ, and it finds both its fulfilment and its eternal security in him.

FOR FURTHER STUDY AND DISCUSSION

1. Discuss some of those elements in the great nations of the past —Greece, Rome, Israel, Germany—that have proved to be destructible.
2. Discuss some of the ways that may lead us as Christians into trouble rather than out of it.
3. Several excellent books are available on the problem of our personal security from the Christian viewpoint. Among them that may be helpful for further study and discussion are: *Faith for Personal Crises,* Carl Michalson; *Personal Security Through Faith,* Lowell Ditzen; *If God Be for Us,* Robert Luccock.
4. Discuss some practical ways of fortifying and building up the inner reserves for spiritual security.

Questions for Review and Written Work

17. List some of the ways in which the church can help you and your community.
18. What can we do to help our church be an effective witness in the world?

Chapter 6

19. Who are the citizens in Christ's kingdom?
20. What are some of the qualities of the citizens of the kingdom of God?
21. Has the kingdom of God come; is it now in the process of coming; or is it to come at some future time?

Chapter 7

22. What do we mean by the "lost provinces" of life?
23. What is the Christian's real vocation?
24. What does the larger stewardship of life include?
25. Whose responsibility is evangelism?

Chapter 8

26. What are some of those things that we may stand to lose in this changing world?
27. When Jesus promised trouble in the world was he thinking primarily of people in general or of his followers?
28. Name some of the crises that develop when we allow trouble to get on the inside.
29. What can we believe that will give abiding and eternal security to life?

Acknowledgments and Copyrights

CONVENTION PRESS acknowledges with gratitude those publishers and individuals who have generously granted permission to use quoted material in this book.

CHAPTER 1

1. Mrs. Billy Graham, "Our Christmas Story," in *The Ladies' Home Journal* (Curtis Publishing Company, December, 1959), p. 59.

2. Frederick Keller Stamm, *I Believe in Man* (Nashville: Abingdon Press, 1959), p. 63.

3. Ralph W. Sockman, *Ours to Use* (New York: Broadcasting and Film Commission, National Council of the Churches of Christ in the United States of America), p. 10.

4. C. B. Caird, *A Primer of Christianity, Part III, The Truth of the Gospel* (London: Oxford University Press, 1950), p. 1.

5. George Arthur Buttrick, ed., *The Interpreter's Bible* (Nashville: Abingdon Press, 1952), I, 467, Walter Russell Bowie, author.

6. Buttrick *op. cit.*, I, 483, Walter Russell Bowie, author.

7. *Ibid.*

8. *Ibid.*

9. E. Y. Mullins, *The Christian Religion in Its Doctrinal Expression* (Kansas City: The Judson Press, 1917), p. 253.

CHAPTER 2

1. W. T. Conner, *Gospel Doctrines* (Nashville: Sunday School Board of the Southern Baptist Convention, 1925), p. 94.

2. W. T. Conner, *The Gospel of Redemption* (Nashville: Broadman Press, 1945), p. 108.

3. George Buttrick, *So We Believe, So We Pray* (Nashville: Abingdon Press, 1951), pp. 97–98.

4. Conner, *op. cit.*, p. 125.

5. Harold W. Tribble, *Our Doctrines* (Nashville: Sunday School Board of the Southern Baptist Convention, 1929), p. 80.

6. Paul Tillich, *The New Being* (New York: Charles Scribner's Sons, Copyright 1955, Paul Tillich), p. 15.

7. Bernhard Citron, *New Birth* (London: Edinburgh University Press, 1951), pp. 20–21.

8. Tillich, *op. cit.*, pp. 19–20.

Chapter 3

1. W. T. Conner, *The Gospel of Redemption* (Nashville: Broadman Press, 1945), p. 139.

2. Samuel Shoemaker, *The Experiment of Faith* (New York: Harper & Brothers, 1957), p. 27.

3. Olive Wyon, *On the Way* (Philadelphia: The Westminster Press, 1958), p. 31.

4. E. Y. Mullins, *The Christian Religion in Its Doctrinal Expression*, p. 417.

5. Wyon, *op. cit.*, p. 42.

6. Donald Craig Kerr, ed., "Design for Christian Living," in *Sermons by Hugh Thomson Kerr* (Philadelphia: Westminster Press, 1953), p. 99.

7. George Arthur Buttrick, ed., *The Interpreter's Bible*, VII, 770, Halford E. Luccock, author.

8. *Ibid.*, p. 455, George Arthur Buttrick, author.

Chapter 4

1. J. B. Phillips, *Making Men Whole* (New York: The Macmillan Co., 1953), pp. 49–50.

2. Margaret Slattery, *One in Seven* (New York: Harper & Brothers, 1939), p. 93.

3. George Buttrick, "The Lonely Prayers of Jesus," a sermon preached on May 20, 1951, at Madison Avenue Presbyterian Church, New York.

Chapter 5

1. W. O. Carver, Introduction to *What Is the Church,* by Duke K. McCall (Nashville: Broadman Press, 1958), p. 6.

2. *Ibid.*, pp. 6, 713.

3. Hugh Thomson Kerr, *Design for Christian Living* (Philadelphia: The Westminster Press, 1953), p. 135.

4. Billy Graham, *Peace with God* (Garden City, New York: Doubleday & Co., Inc., 1953), p. 176.

5. Charles Rann Kennedy, *The Servant in the House* (New York: Harper and Brothers, 1908), pp. 67–68.

6. Elmer G. Homrighausen, *I Believe in the Church* (Nashville: Abingdon Press, 1959), p. 68.

7. Robert McCracken, "The Vocation of the Church," a sermon preached in the Riverside Church, New York, October 6, 1946.

8. Harold A. Bosley, *The Church Militant* (New York: Harper & Brothers, 1952), p. 134.

9. Robert E. Luccock, *If God Be for Us* (New York: Harper & Brothers, 1954), p. 149.

Chapter 6

1. James S. Stewart, *The Life and Teaching of Jesus Christ* (Nashville: Abingdon Press, 1958), p. 53.

2. John Bright, *The Kingdom of God* (Nashville: Abingdon Press, 1953), p. 187.

3. George Arthur Buttrick, ed., *The Interpreter's Bible,* VII, 329–330, George Arthur Buttrick, author.

4. W. T. Conner, *The Gospel of Redemption,* p. 294.

5. Bright, *op. cit.*, pp. 233–234.

6. *Ibid.*, p. 244.

7. *Ibid.*, p. 218.

Chapter 7

1. Elton Trueblood, *Your Other Vocation* (New York: Harper & Brothers, 1952), p. 27.

2. Ibid., pp. 31–32.

3. Ibid., p. 32.

4. Simeon Stylites Column, "Money Changers in the Temple," *The Christian Century* (Chicago, July 27, 1960), p. 887.

5. *Ibid.*

6. "From 'Mission' to 'Missions,'" Editorial, *Christianity Today* (Washington, August 1, 1960), p. 20.

7. *Ibid.*

8. Donald G. Miller, *The Nature and Mission of the Church* (Richmond: John Knox Press, 1957), p. 71.

Chapter 8

1. Robert E. Luccock, *If God Be for Us,* p. 126.

2. *Ibid.*, pp. 43–44.

3. Harold Blake Walker, *Power to Manage Yourself* (New York: Harper & Brothers, 1955), p. 122.

4. Carl Michalson, *Faith for Personal Crises* (New York: Charles Scribner's Sons, (© 1958, Southwestern University), pp. 139–140.

5. Harry Emerson Fosdick, *A Faith for Tough Times* (New York: Harper & Brothers, 1952), p. 28.

6. George Matheson, *Studies of the Portrait of Christ,* quoted in *The Pulpit,* September, 1960 (Doubleday & Co., Inc.), pp. 5–6.

7. Joseph Fort Newton, *His Cross and Ours* (New York: Harper & Brothers, 1941), p. 23.

8. James D. Smart, *What a Man Can Believe* (Philadelphia: The Westminster Press, 1943), pp. 235–236.